To Don Mc Namee

A good friend and
superb cataloger!

With affection,

Jeanne T. Freeman

CHECK OUT A LIBRARIAN

by
Johanna E. Tallman

The Scarecrow Press, Inc.
Metuchen, N.J., & London
1985

Library of Congress Cataloging-in-Publication Data
Tallman, Johanna E., 1914-

    Check out a librarian.
    "Writings by Johanna E. Tallman": p.
    Includes index.
    1. Tallman, Johanna E., 1914- . 2. Librarians
--United States--Biography. 3. Library science.
I. Title.
Z720.T36A33 1985   020'.92'4 [B]   85-10845
ISBN 0-8108-1823-X

I gratefully acknowledge my sister,

Helene E. Stevens,

for assistance in editing the manuscript

CONTENTS

v

vi

DEDICATION

This book is dedicated to colleague, mentor and friend Law-rence Clark Powell, famed author, bibliophile, raconteur, educator, library administrator, dean and librarian.

We met in 1936 while we were both students at the School of Librarianship at the University of California, Berkeley. He had already been "out in the world" and had his doctoral degree, and the rest of us looked up to him. After graduation he soon rose in the library world, and by 1944 he became the University Librarian at the University of California, Los Angeles (1944-1961).

When he agreed to hire me as the Engineering Librarian in 1945, we began a long collaboration in the development of the system of branch libraries and in the establishment of the School of Library Service at UCLA. He said, "You are in charge. Do what you think is best. I will not interfere unless I receive a complaint about you." Apparently he never did.

Powell treated me and other members of his staff as responsible colleagues. Senior librarians were invited to be members of his Administrative Council, where he encouraged them to speak out and participate. I can still hear him saying at some of the meetings: "Jo, what do YOU think about this? You haven't said anything yet."

As the head of a library system myself in later years, I tried to emulate his type of leadership:

● Treat every staff member, from the lowest clerk to

the highest assistant, with friendliness and respect, as a part of the library team.

- Keep lines of communication open. Be available. Listen. Seek input from senior staff, not only from Assistant University Librarians.

- Give responsibility to those who qualify. Encourage them to plan ahead, to learn newer techniques, to grow in the profession.

- Establish good relations with your superiors, the faculty, colleagues in other libraries, professional organizations, and your public. You need them, and let them know that they need you.

Thank you, Larry, for the long-lasting inspiration you provided during the years.

Johanna E. Tallman
September 1984

INTRODUCTION

Do you think librarians read all the time? Lead a quiet, uninvolved life? Check out books to readers? Go around saying "Shhhhhhh!"? If you do, here is your opportunity to check out a librarian. Professional librarians are busy, informed people, who enjoy providing a specialized service called INFORMATION. In their work they have amusing, unusual and occasionally scary experiences. Find out some of the interesting and exciting events in the life of one of them over the nearly fifty years of her career.

I have also included stories relating to my six-month stay in Brazil, where I went on a Fulbright grant. There was "culture shock" involved, as shown in some of these descriptions.

Readers will discover a variety of fascinating experiences, stemming from unusual questions asked by library patrons, unique research problems posed by movie producers and professors, and contacts with inquisitive, and sometimes difficult, persons. After you have read these stories, visit and "check out" a few librarians. They can be fun, and--believe it or not--they're human!

PART I:

FOLLOWING AND CREATING OPPORTUNITIES; AN AUTOBIOGRAPHICAL RESUME

STARTING IN THE PROFESSION, 1928-1937

While attending a small private high school, the school librarian asked me if I would like to help a little. I did, and gradually became more involved. When she left during my senior year, I was asked to take charge of the library while finishing school, an opportunity which started me on my career.

By this time I was seriously considering becoming a professional librarian. Through a family acquaintance I obtained an appointment with the head of the Los Angeles Public Library, Althea Warren. She urged me to get my bachelor's degree and then apply to the best graduate library school in the West, the School of Librarianship at the University of California, Berkeley. I followed her advice and gained admittance to this school, which had an enrollment limited to fifty.

Graduating in 1937, during the Depression, meant limited job opportunities. For the first month I worked for an uncle who was in the real estate business. Then I learned that the School of Librarianship was to offer summer school courses in cataloging and reference work, at the University of California, Los Angeles (UCLA). I inquired about any job openings. Yes, there was a part-time position assisting the professors. In order to provide a full semester of credit, the classes were taught six days a week for seven weeks. For my part-time help for this time I was paid a total of

Johanna Tallman at time of graduation from the School of Librarianship, 1937.

$45! At least this was an opportunity to get some post-graduate experience.

In September I learned of an opening in the San Marino Public Library. (San Marino, a city of wealthy residents, is where the Huntington Library is located.) The position was as assistant librarian, responsible for cataloging new books. The previous assistant had worked for $90 per month. The management wanted to raise the pay, but, not having the extra amount in the budget, offered me the position at a monthly rate of $90 for six-hour days. I took it, with the understanding that I could leave at any time to accept a full-time position.

A SPECIALTY EMERGES, 1938-1944

The following January I took a civil service examination for the Los Angeles County Public Library (not the Los Angeles City Library) and passed high enough to be hired as a junior librarian. The pay was $115 a month, but required a forty-four-hour work week. Here I worked first in the Branches Division, selecting books from the basic stock in the main library to fill out the holdings in the branch libraries, preparing reading lists, etc. I advanced to the Catalog Department where, among other tasks, I recataloged all of the Spanish surname books, most of which had been entered incorrectly in the catalog. My high school Spanish was paying off.

One day the County Librarian, Helen Vogleson, said she wanted to transfer me to the Reference Department to help the Technical Reference Librarian, Eugene D. Hart. I demurred, saying I didn't know much about technical or scientific subjects or the related literature. But she replied that I could learn and she felt I could do the job. So began what turned out to be the start of my long career as a science and technology literature specialist.

At that time the County Library served approximately 600,000 residents in 23 municipalities and all the unincorporated areas of the county. There were 134 community branch libraries and 80 school branches. All of the professional library work was done at the headquarters in downtown Los Angeles. The Technical Reference Librarian was responsible for selecting books in science and technology for the larger branch libraries, answering subject requests mailed in by library patrons, making surveys of technical subject fields, and handling related tasks.

This position required thorough knowledge of scientific and technical literature and reference sources, and acquaintance with the special interests of the residents of these communities. With the questioner miles away and his or her request reduced to a few words on a 3" x 5" form, the librarian had to use imagination, resourcefulness and "leg work" to understand the request, and check the card catalog, periodical indexes, lists of government documents, and tables of contents of books listed in publishers' catalogs to find the best information.

On the first day in the Reference Department I had to find answers to questions involving the following variety of subjects: Chinese herb (Fu-ti-tieng), ice-cream freezing for commercial purposes, gardenia growing, ulcers of the stomach, reading weather reports, specifications for concrete in the city of Los Angeles, gold and where you find it, and Pythagorean numbers.

When Mr. Hart resigned a year later to accept a better position elsewhere, I was appointed acting Technical Reference Librarian, pending results of a countrywide civil service examination which was expected to provide another male librarian (a status symbol at the time) from the industrial Midwest or the East Coast. None of the seven men, in the total of forty-five applicants who took the written examination, came close to the top three. After the oral interviews where over, I came out on top, and Miss Vogleson rather reluctantly appointed the female home talent already on her staff. Civil service overrode any prejudices, allowing equal opportunity in 1939.

This was the period of "National Defense," and Los Angeles County was expanding rapidly in airplane manufacture, shipbuilding, and related activities, such as civilian defense. Libraries were swamped with requests for technical books and information, as reflected in requests reaching the Central Library. During the year 1941/42 the technical reference staff handled 3,645 mail requests.

Early in 1942 Mr. Hart returned to the Los Angeles area to head up the Pacific Aeronautical Library, and newly established central library facility for the aircraft companies. It had been founded the year before and was located in Hollywood. Mr. Hart asked me to join him as the assistant librarian. I decided this was a new opportunity to extend my contact with the specialized technical literature used by aeronautical engineers. Since I knew it would probably take awhile for the County Library to go through the civil service process to find a replacement, I gave Miss Vogleson four months' notice.

She called me into her office, an inner sanctum seldom seen by the regular staff.

"You have been unethical," she announced.

"What have I done?" I asked with some trepidation.

"You did not ask for my permission to resign. I will blackball you throughout California."

"But I didn't know I had to do that," I stammered, and slunk out of the office.

What to do? I recalled that the California Library Association had recently passed a code of practice, and I looked up a copy. It stated that it was not necessary to ask permission of your employer to leave (which apparently had been the custom). All that was required was to give notice equivalent to the length of the annual vacation. In my case that was two weeks.

I wrote Miss Vogleson a letter, quoting the code:

If the candidate is employed in another institution, negotiations may be opened directly with the individual under consideration. He should notify his Chief Librarian immediately upon appointment.

I felt free to leave. From that day to the day she died, she never spoke to me again.

At a later occasion I had an opportunity to talk to the State Librarian, Mabel Gillis, and asked if Miss Vogleson had tried to blackball me. "No, she didn't," she replied. "But if she had, we wouldn't have paid any attention. She was always making threats like that to keep good employees from leaving." So it was really a roundabout compliment! I forgave her long ago because it was she who had insisted I could be a technical reference librarian, and thus provided me with a major opportunity to develop my special career.

While I was waiting to start my new position, Mr.
Hart and I collaborated on putting together a reading list,
Training for War. As World War II began, libraries all
over the country were besieged by people who wanted to get
into industries related to the war effort. This publication
listed books in such fields as aeronautical training, civil
defense, industrial management, industrial training, military
and naval science, and shipbuilding and marine engineering.
The list was published as a supplement to the American Library Association Booklist (see Reference 1), so that libraries
throughout the country could have access to it.

In July 1942 I became the Assistant Librarian at the
Pacific Aeronautical Library. This library was opened in
October 1941 through the cooperation of the Institute of the
Aeronautical Sciences--a national scientific organization--
and several of the large local aircraft companies. Its establishment was the direct result of agitation on the part of a
group of special and public librarians who realized the need
for a centralized research library for the aircraft industry
in Southern California. The library served fifteen libraries
in Los Angeles County, as well as two libraries in San Diego.

Soon the library was put under the active supervision
of the Aircraft War Production Council, an organization com-
posed of the presidents of the seven largest aircraft companies
on the Pacific Coast. This council coordinated such war-
time matters as personnel and equipment.

Services originated by Mr. Hart included these:

1. The daily delivery of books and journals by a
   messenger in a van (called "Speedee"), covering
   a round trip of 150 miles -- a pioneer library
   network system! This was in the days before
   photocopies, and public and academic libraries
   were reluctant to loan magazines for a long period
   of time. However, by providing a turn-around
   time of two days, we were able to borrow material
   for our users.

2. A regularly issued catalog card index, with abstracts, of current technical articles of aeronautic
   interest. These were duplicated on a multilith
   machine (more sophisticated than a mimeograph),
   and sent to nineteen libraries, including the Library of Congress Division of Aeronautics and
   the Institute of the Aeronautical Sciences in New York.

3. The indexing and distribution of cards for engineering reports which the various aircraft companies made available to each other for informational purposes while the war lasted. (For additional information, see Reference 2)

In September 1942 Mr. Hart, a reserve officer in the U. S. Army, was called to active duty. After the interim tenure of another librarian, I was appointed as the head of this special library.

My affiliation with Gene Hart lasted only a short time, but it was he who guided me in the techniques and sources for locating technical information, in devising special services for special users, and in writing effective reports. I could not have asked for a better "mentor" at the start of my career as a technical librarian.

TAKING CHARGE OF A NEW LIBRARY, 1945-1946

As early as June 1943 I read an announcement in the newspaper about the proposed establishment of an aeronautical engineering school at UCLA. I wrote to then University Librarian John E. Goodwin and said that in the event an aeronautical library was to be organized and a trained and experienced librarian would be needed, I would like to be considered for the position. He replied briefly that it was too soon to consider such a position, since the school itself had not yet been funded by the State Legislature.

In the summer of 1944 World War II was drawing to a close. The aircraft companies decided they wanted libraries of their own and no longer wished to share their research. They were looking ahead to peacetime competition. The Aircraft War Production Council (which had been the coordinating agency for the aircraft industry in manpower, the Pacific Aeronautical Library and other matters) decided that its function would soon be eliminated. The library staff was reduced from $8\frac{1}{2}$ to 5 (F. T. E.). I decided to seek a more permanent position in a growing library.

By this time Mr. Goodwin had retired at UCLA and been replaced by Dr. Lawrence Clark Powell. He had been a distinguished classmate of mine in the School of Librarianship at Berkeley. Once again I thought of the pro-

posed aeronautical engineering school and the opportunity to
get in on the ground floor as its librarian.   I wrote to Dr.
Powell about the possibility of such a job.

This time the response was quick: "Come out to
UCLA and see the new dean of engineering who has just
arrived.   If he goes along with the idea of an engineering
librarian, we'll work something out."

I made an appointment with Dean L.M.K. Boelter.
He was enthusiastic about getting a library started right away
and thought my qualifications were just right.   He urged me
to visit the engineering library at the University of California
at Berkeley, for some perspective on such a library in an
academic setting.   I took his advice and spent two weeks
with the librarian, Blanche H. Dalton.

With the support of Dean Boelter, Dr. Powell arranged
for me to be appointed to an available senior-grade position
in the Reference Department of the University Library, effective January 2, 1945.   The salary was to be $165 a month,
plus an emergency $25 a month paid to all employees re-
ceiving less than $300 a month.

At that time the university budget operated on a bi-
ennial schedule, and there were eighteen months to go before
the new position of engineering librarian could be created.
In the meantime, I would work about half-time in the general
reference room and the rest of the time collaborate with
Dean Boelter in the preliminary organization of a branch
engineering library.   Thus began my twenty-eight years of
fruitful service at UCLA.

Dean Boelter explained that he had gone to the aircraft companies and asked what kind of engineers they might
want.   "We don't want any aerodynamicists since we can get
all we want from Caltech.   What we want are engineers who
are all around capable of doing anything we might get into
in the post-war era.   We DON'T want the old style of civil,
electrical or mechanical engineers!"

The Dean thereupon changed the name of the school
to the College of Engineering, dropping "aeronautical."   He
subsequently developed the idea of a core curriculum that
all beginning students would be required to take.   In their
upper division and graduate years, the students would then
go into specialties.   The success of his ideas and the school

he created are reflected in the distinguished alumni of the school and the very high standing which the school developed and retains to this day.

Although I served half of each day at the Main Library Reference Desk, the rest of the time was spent at a small desk getting started on the Engineering Library.

How does one start a new library "from scratch"? What would we need in the way of books, journals, technical reports? Space? Personnel? Equipment? Procedures?

A library begins its existence when it begins to acquire a collection of relevant publications. My first task was to ascertain what subjects were to be taught and to search the main library book stacks to see what might be there that could be transferred. (There wasn't much.) The Dean and I went through technical book publishers' catalogs looking for pertinent titles.

Initially I showed my selections to the Dean, but after several weeks he said, "You seem to know what you're doing. So go ahead, and just check with me if you have any questions." Eventually we established a faculty library advisory committee and I could consult with it on difficult choices.

While getting started on the collection, I did not overlook the other questions. I drew up a planning document, trying to envision what the library would be like in five, ten, or twenty-five years. Dean Boelter suggested even fifty years!

A mere collection does not become a working library until it is organized for use. My second task, then, was to plan the records and cataloging that would organize the growing collection for its most effective use. I was aware that this was the first branch library, although small departmental libraries, such as Chemistry and Geology, had existed for many years. In essence, the difference was that a branch library was to be a growing collection, containing all of the publications available on campus in that subject, rather than merely a small and static working collection of the most important books and journals culled from the collection in the main library.

A branch library was to have a complete card catalog of its holdings, and its staff was part of the University

Library staff rather than of the school or department. The
aim was to give these branch libraries more professional
supervision and the opportunity to develop into real service
outlets, rather than mere storage and self-service units.

To accomplish these aims meant a new approach by
all concerned to library organization and management. Some
of the traditional procedures by which departmental libraries
had been run had to be upset. "But we have always done
it this other way" was the protesting argument when changes
were suggested. It took patience, logical argument, and assurance of support from above to surmount these obstacles.
The most important skirmish, which took several years to
settle, was the matter of subject cataloging (which I will discuss later, in Part II).

Other innovations were also needed to streamline procedures. At that time books in departmental libraries were
not so designated in the University Library card catalog. A
person who found the desired book listed in the catalog would
write down the book call number and then head for the huge
library book stacks. Not finding the book on the shelf, the
searcher would then proceed to the circulation desk. There
an attendant would go through the files and finally find a
"dummy" charge card under that number, with the notation
"Chemistry Library," or "Geology Library," etc.

As soon as I became aware of this cumbersome system,
I suggested that the card catalog show the name of the branch
library and not just the call number. Then the library user
would need to know only where the branch library was located
and be on the way.

"I realize that this system may work for the small
departmental libraries," I said to the head of the Circulation
Department. "But do you really want a hundred thousand
dummy circulation cards to sit in your files?"

"Well, no," she conceded. "That's a lot!"

"So let's dispense with those for the Engineering Library," I announced. "We're going to become a large library. When other professional school branch libraries come
along, we should have a useful system in place."

These changes were agreed to.

Another problem was with the checking done to verify the correct author, title, publisher, date, price, etc. for books to be ordered. Although my growing staff and I did careful work, all of the information was re-checked by the Bibliographical Checking Section of the Order Department before going on to the Order Writing Section.

"Don't you trust our information?" I asked. "Why can't we send our slips directly to the Order Writing Section to speed up our orders? If we should make a mistake, we'll take the blame." I won that one, also.

As time went by we pressed for more changes to avoid duplication of work and to speed procedures for the new professional school branch libraries that were being established -- Biomedical, Law, Management, Education, and others. Journals were to be sent directly to branch libraries instead of being routed and checked in by the Serials Section. After several years, it was agreed that books could be ordered from dealers or publishers directly instead of through the Order Department.

Eventually the cataloging processing was also turned over to the largest of these branch libraries. We had become an integral wedge in the library "pie," and not just a satellite spinning somewhere outside.

LIBRARY SPACE PLANNING, 1946-1959

Where to put the growing collection? By June 1945 we were given a small storage area in which we could put a reading table, shared by students. There were some shelves for storage space in lieu of desk drawers, but no room for a desk. It was still difficult in this immediate post-war era to obtain such equipment as typewriters and oak or steel shelving, so we "made do" with wooden planks and whatever odds and ends of card catalogs and equipment we could salvage from other sources.

As time went by, we expanded into the adjacent newspaper storage area until we could encroach no more. We all knew that the basic principle of library space -- LIBRARIES GROW -- would soon catch up.

In preparation for planning a more permanent library,

I was sent by the University on a trip to see other engineering libraries. I visited the University of Illinois Engineering Library; Northwestern Technological Institute, in Evanston, Illinois; the National Safety Council Library; the University of Chicago; Rensselaer Polytechnic Institute (the first engineering school in the United States); City College of New York; New York University; Columbia University; Institute of the Aeronautical Sciences; Harvard University; and the Massachusetts Institute of Technology. Librarians were impressed that a branch librarian of a barely existent library was subsidized to go on such an extensive trip.

But it paid off. Everywhere I went I observed library layout, equipment, files, staffing and other details. And I discovered many shortcomings and tips on what and what not to do.

In August 1948 the Engineering Library moved into a larger area on the top floor of the west wing of what is now known as the Powell Library. This was the same area where I had my first post-graduate job in 1937.

In this new location I was, at last, able to have a real desk. The shelving, tables and chairs were from the pre-War Graduate Reading Room. Hardly had we settled in when we were told to share the room equally with the newly revived Graduate Reading Room, which was anticipating its new quarters in the east wing. It was a unique experience to have our rather boisterous, phone-jangling, busy atmosphere in the same room as the sedate, studious and quiet one which the other librarian was trying to foster in her half of the room.

During this time the Board of Regents of the university held one of its meetings in the newly constructed east wing, in what was to become the new Graduate Reading Room. We were alerted to keep our telephones clear in case there was an incoming call for one of the Regents, as ours was the nearest telephone. One of the Regents was Admiral Chester Nimitz. When he arrived at the Main Reading Room he went up to the Reference Desk and asked where the meeting was to take place. One of the librarians said courteously:

"I'll be glad to show you," and started coming out from behind the counter.

"Do not desert your post, young lady!" he said sternly. "Just tell me where it is. I'll be able to find it!"

After the Graduate Reading Room was moved out we hardly had time to enjoy the full use of the room again before sundry workers arrived with steel partitions, jack hammers, and wall smashers, to install a series of faculty study offices along one wall. All our equipment had to be moved toward the inner part of the room.

I'll never forget the experience of trying to maintain "normal" service with the cold breezes blowing through the wide-open windows, the smell of wet plaster, and sound of jack hammers biting into concrete, the confusion of rehanging the study doors (because "in" on the specifications had been interpreted as "into" the offices, when it should have been "into" the larger reading room), and the sawing of lumber to make wedges to bring office partitions up to level on the sagging floor.

After seven months of construction and confusion, the offices and new walls were finally completed, and we began to share our space with ten professorial tenants, some silent and unseen, others gregarious and active. One of the professors carefully measured the space in each office and found that the end one nearest the entrance had four inches more in width. Thereupon he demanded to have that one.

Additional faculty study offices were approved and, in January 1952, it finally became necessary to move the library to its next temporary home, on the fourth floor of the original Engineering Building. A few years later a small room across the hall was added. We remained in that area until 1959.

In 1957 plans were started for a large new engineering building which was to include the permanent home for the Engineering Library. As a result of my library visiting trip I insisted on meeting on a regular basis with the architects. We selected the top floor for two major reasons: 1) it would allow the main reading room to be constructed without columns, which are always a nuisance in laying out a library; 2) it was away from the main traffic, so that those who made it up to the eighth floor would come to use the library and not just to pass a few minutes between classes.

There were three stack levels and a full elevator to serve all floors. The west side was designed with knock-out walls, so that eventually the library could be extended by building four levels over an existing auditorium. Before

I left UCLA in 1973 I prepared detailed plans for carrying out this expansion, but money to build this has not yet been provided.

One problem surfaced just as we were about to move in July 1959. I discovered that the shelves in the new library were too short from front to back for our technical books. I had specified nine-inch shelves. When I reported this problem to the architect, he checked and found that someone had ordered "standard" shelving, which is eight inches. At first the manufacturer's representative said: "We sent what you ordered," but soon he reported that he had just received an order from a public library which wanted standard shelves. He would take our wrong size shelves off our hands and pay the University 10¢ on the dollar. Since they had also hung too many shelves (I had specified six shelves per section and they had installed seven), we had an excess number of shelves to turn in, so the loss was not quite so staggering.

EXPANDING COLLECTIONS AND RESPONSIBILITIES, 1959-1973

By 1959 the staff of the Engineering Library had grown to nine -- four librarians and five clerks, augmented by student assistants. The book collection totalled about 39,000 volumes and was growing at the rate of nearly 4,000 books per year. Nearly 47,000 publications were circulated during the year.

The Meteorology Departmental Library was integrated with the Engineering Library when the latter moved into its larger space in 1959. Soon the astronomy and mathematics books from the main library were also scheduled to be transferred. It was time to consider a change in name for the library.

A committee of faculty members representing the departments was appointed to look into this. I pointed out that it would be impractical for our staff to answer the telephone with "Engineering, Astronomy, Mathematics and Meteorology Library." The mathematics professor said, "Mathematics is the pure science. Therefore it should be 'Mathematics, Engineering, Astronomy and Meteorology Library.'"

Finally I said, "The Engineering Library is the largest component of this collection. Your three departments [Astronomy, Mathematics and Meteorology] have already agreed to call the building where your offices are housed the Mathematical Sciences Building. So why don't we call this the 'Engineering and Mathematical Sciences Library'?" A vote was taken and the name was adopted, with the dissent of the mathematics professor. Our vote was forwarded to the University Librarian who concurred with the majority.

At first it was difficult for our staff to give the fuller name when answering the telephone. One day a staff member said, "Engineering Library." The voice at the other end said, rather sarcastically: "Isn't this the Engineering and MATHEMATICAL SCIENCES Library?" We soon learned to say all the words. For short reference we used "E.M.S. Library."

The integration of other collections into a library is not just a matter of the physical move from one location to another. Material is moved from one identified location to a differently identified location. All pertinent records, such as catalog cards for books and magazine listings, must be changed. For us the year 1962/63 was called "The Year of the Transfer Program," when some 4,900 volumes were formally transferred.

In November 1962 I was appointed Coordinator of the Physical Sciences Libraries. In addition to the E.M.S. Library, these were Chemistry, Geology/Geophysics and Physics libraries. The original problems concerned final plans for new or expanded space in each library, expediting the ordering of books by the Main Library, and surveying personnel and budget needs.

These libraries had been clamoring to have better and faster cataloging of their incoming books. It was decided that the staff of the E.M.S. Library should handle the cataloging for these branches in addition to its own collection. So, starting in July 1964, we began the integration and centralization of ordering and cataloging services for all of these libraries.

Soon after we began this new service I had a call from a physics professor. "I want to put a book on reserve [limited lending] in the Physics Library. I know it takes a long time to order a book and get it cataloged. I want to give you the title now so the book will be ready by the time school begins in the fall."

I gave the author and title of the book to my acquisitions librarian, with instructions to go to Westwood Village
(adjacent to the University) and try to find a copy. When he
came back with it, I gave it to the cataloger, asking her to
catalog it immediately. By three o'clock it was ready.

I called the professor and said, somewhat casually:
"The reserve book you ordered is ready. Shall I send it
over right away to the Physics Library?" He was stunned.
"But I gave it to you only this morning! How can you have
it ready this afternoon?" "We are prepared to give you this
kind of service," I responded rather proudly.

By 1973 my staff had grown to nineteen, including a
cataloging staff of six. There were ten more employees in
the other three libraries. The total number of books in the
E.M.S. Library had grown to nearly 132,000; circulation for
the year reached nearly 61,000 items. The E.M.S. Library
also contained 6,343 serial titles then currently received,
81,500 microcards, 430,547 microfiches, 2,727 microfilm
reels, 108,754 technical reports (full-size, unbound), and
2,257 cataloged pamphlets.

Aside from being a useful collection for the schools
and departments the library served at UCLA, the collections
were increasingly used by other libraries. During 1972/73
the E.M.S. Library received 2,652 interlibrary loan requests,
of which 1,785 were filled. On the other hand, the E.M.S.
Library requested only 263 items from other libraries. The
reference staff handled 17,333 information and reference requests that year.

We had come a long way!

IT'S TIME FOR A CHANGE, 1971-1973

In early 1971 I asked University Librarian Robert
Vosper for my reclassification to the title of Assistant University Librarian, a title which had been accorded to the
Biomedical and Law Librarians. I felt that my many contributions to the University Library system were at least
as significant. He responded by saying that if I could bring
in two first-rate job offers to show my professional attraction
to other employers, he would see what he could do for me.

I lined up and interviewed for two such positions, one as the Director of Libraries of a national laboratory near Chicago, and the other as Assistant University Librarian at the University of California, Riverside. This latter position was in fact equivalent to mine at UCLA, but on a smaller scale, coordinating the physical sciences libraries on that campus. At least that institution was willing to give the Assistant University Librarian designation to this position.

When I reported these two higher positions to the University Librarian, he said, "Why don't you accept one of them?" He did not offer to follow through on his promise to see what he could do for me at UCLA. I really had no desire to move to Chicago environs or to Riverside, so I stayed to wait for something better to develop closer to home.

Reflecting later on this episode, I came to realize that this suggestion to apply for other jobs to enhance one's local position is not professionally proper, since the interviewers assume that the applicant is a bona fide prospect. I regretted that, at the time, I had not seen the suggestion in that light.

In April 1973 I received a call from Professor Rodman Paul, Chairman of the Library Director Search Committee at the California Institute of Technology in nearby Pasadena. He asked if I would be willing to be a consultant to advise the Committee on the future of the Caltech libraries and the selection of a new Director of Libraries.

I agreed and then spent one day surveying various departments in the library, discussing the library with the Vice-Provost, having lunch with the Committee, back to the library for more observations, and finally meeting with the Committee to give them my preliminary impressions. This was followed later by a fuller written analysis of my comments and recommendations.

At the end of the day Professor Paul asked, "Would you consider applying for the position of Director of Libraries? We are impressed with your qualifications and would like to consider you."

I thought it over for a few days. My husband had passed away a year before and I felt that a change of location would be good for me. Also, I had been at UCLA for over twenty-eight years. A change of responsibilities and challenges would be exciting. A week later I wrote to Professor Paul:

> Since my meeting with you I have given considerable
> thought to the possibility of my applying for the
> position of Director of Libraries. I have compared
> the challenge and satisfaction of that position with
> the one at UCLA [Planning Officer for the University
> Library, a new position for which I had also applied].
> Both are high level and prestigious and both will re-
> quire a high degree of application to solving tremen-
> dous problems. But, on reflection, it seems to
> me that the position at Caltech has more all around
> appeal and fits better into my experience and inter-
> ests. I believe it offers more contact with people.
> The whole milieu is on a less grandiose scale. The
> feeling of pride in the Institute and its Library is
> noticeable in the contacts I have had. The concept
> of operating within more clearly defined objectives
> is also appealing. I believe my many years of
> professional and administrative experience, mostly
> with science-technical literature and libraries,
> qualify me to undertake the position of Director....

In a few days I had his response:

> ... We will give most serious consideration to your
> application. The impression you made on our li-
> brary staff was heartwarming. We won't be able
> to make a decision until we have completed inter-
> views with two, possibly three, candidates with whom
> we are already in correspondence....

Then began a wait of about one month. Finally Professor Paul called and said that I was the choice and would
receive an official offer by mail. This came from the Vice-
Provost.

As soon as I heard the news I did two things: I wrote
a letter of acceptance and then called a real estate agent to
sell my house and help me find another one close to Pasadena.
The final word was a letter from (then) President Harold
Brown:

> I take pleasure in notifying you officially the Board
> of Trustees appointed you Director of Libraries....
> This action was taken upon the recommendation of
> a special Search Committee and the Vice-Provost
> and with the approval of the Provost and the Presi-
> dent.... We are looking forward to welcoming

you to Pasadena and are delighted over the pro-
spects of your joining our staff.

After winding up my affairs at UCLA, selling my
home, and relocating closer to Pasadena, I began my new
career on August 1, 1973.

CLIMAX OF THE CAREER, 1973-1981

On the day I arrived in my new position at the California Institute of Technology (Caltech), I found a note on
the desk blotter: "Please write the annual report." This
is certainly a useful way to obtain an overall picture of what
has happened during the previous year. After reviewing reports from the last few years I realized that some statistics
needed redefining and updating. Years of experience in com-
piling such reports had alerted me to both trouble spots and
ways of presenting a useful and readable report. I finished
this one fairly quickly and turned to more pressing matters.

It did not take me long to ascertain that there would
not be enough money to pay for periodical subscription re-
newals. The prices for science and technical journals were
rising faster than the cost of living, especially for foreign
publications. My analysis showed we would need another
$70,000 that year to get by. But to have money allocated
in the middle of the fiscal year is not easy. We received
half. It was too late to cancel subscriptions for that year,
so all we could do was stop buying books and use that money
to pay the subscriptions.

We managed to squeak by that year, but built a case
for a bigger budget the next year. Some money could be
saved by cutting back duplicate subscriptions, of which there
were quite a few because of the many separate campus libraries.

One way to save money is by cooperating with other
libraries. This can be done through borrowing on interlibrary loan, cooperative buying ("You buy that and we'll
buy this"), or arranging for your library users to go to other
libraries. Such a system had been worked out with UCLA
and the University of Southern California (USC) through a
consortium called CALINET. A van makes daily trips be-

California Institute of Technology, Pasadena, California,
showing the Millikan Memorial (Library Building) at right.
San Gabriel Mountains are in the background.

tween these institutions, some days favoring trips from Caltech to UCLA and USC and alternate days favoring students
from those campuses to come to Caltech. The van also car-
ries interlibrary loan books, intercampus mail (through a
permissible regulation of the U.S. Postal Service), faculty
and students attending cooperative classes and, occasionally,
laboratory specimens, such as mice or blood for the Biology
Department.

(For an article on cooperative academic libraries
feasibility, see Reference 46. For information on budget
coping, see Reference 53. For a review of interlibrary
loans as related to new copyright regulations, see References 59 and 63.)

Problems presenting unusual challenges surfaced quickly
in the chief library building called the Robert Andrews Millikan Memorial. The word "Library" does not appear on the

building's sign. The original plans for a library building provided for a wide structure four or five stories high, suitable for library purposes. But the donor insisted on a tower as a memorial to Dr. Millikan, Nobel Prize winner in physics (1923) and President of Caltech during its important formative years in the 1920's. A nine-story tower was erected (and subsequently was used as a locale for a "Mission: Impossible" episode). Each floor is about 80 feet square, but the center is taken up by an enclosed core for two elevators, two rest rooms, a stairwell and a janitor's closet. This leaves only about 25 feet between the inner and outer walls on each side, to accommodate offices, library shelves and aisles. It's like a square doughnut, with the hole representing nonusable library space. Supervision of any floor is impossible. In a faculty survey of library service, the building received negative votes and comments from nearly everyone. When I invited my predecessor to visit some time, he wrote: "I will never enter that atrocious building again!"

To provide more shelf space for a growing collection, we added shelves in aisles, replaced low shelves with high ones, converted some reading space and finally stored older material in former branch libraries which had been converted to reading rooms.

By combining the cataloging staff of the Humanities and Social Sciences Library with the rest of the Catalog Department, we utilized the released space to create much needed room for a microform center, with microform (microfilm and microfiche) readers, printers, and cabinets for a growing collection of books, newspapers and journals in microform.

Instead of permitting a variety of check-out circulation methods on each floor, we centralized the circulation process on the ground floor for better control. But such innovation did not happen without a struggle. The individual libraries on each floor had used cards of various shapes and with different wording. There were several loan periods -- one day, one week, two weeks, etc. Even persuading the librarians from the upper floor libraries to agree on some basic rules took awhile. I designed a new style uniform charge card which could be sorted for overdues, after learning that overdue notices had not been sent out routinely, if at all. I discovered that some professors had material charged out thirteen years ago! When I suggested that these library books were no longer available for general use and that, if professors wanted to keep books indefinitely, they should purchase them, I was greeted with disbelief. They were simply not used to that point of view.

The revised charge cards were designed to be photocopied for overdue notices. The name and address of the borrower could be read in window envelopes, thus avoiding the need to address the envelopes. This meant that for each borrowing transaction a new card would have to be filled out, a normal procedure carried out in hundreds of libraries. But one professor was completely opposed to any change from what he had been used to:

"You mean I have to fill in a card for each book I want to take out?!"

"Well," I offered, "while you are filling in one card our staff member can fill in another, ready for your signature."

He stormed out. Soon a petition arrived from him and some of his colleagues, demanding that I go back to the old system, and threatening to have me fired! I asked the professor to discuss the matter in my office.

"I am a trained academic librarian with years of experience," I told him. "I don't tell you how to teach, so don't tell me how to run a library."

When I reported this matter to my superior, he calmed me and said that he would handle the professor. "You know we have a lot of prima donnas here." Eventually the professor cooperated with our system.

Of course, many libraries now have on-line computerized circulation procedures which are very quick. But this takes elaborate preparation and expensive handling and equipment. The circulation handled at that check-out desk was quite small -- about 32,000 items per year -- and would not justify the extraordinary expense of an automated system.

Another related problem was that the library used both the Dewey Decimal Classification and the Library of Congress Classification System. (See "Order Out of Chaos.") When the Humanities and Social Sciences Library began to grow quickly in the later 1960's, the staff had opted to use the L.C. system for their new acquisitions. For many years

I had known that the L.C. system was much better for academic libraries, and so I started a modest recataloging program to bring the science libraries and the reference collection into this system. It would be inexpedient to put the old Dewey records into a computer for a circulation program, if the next week, month, or year those records would have to be deleted and new L.C. records inserted.

However, we did go into on-line cataloging by signing up with a nationwide cataloging consortium, called OCLC. A related on-line computer service was RLIN (Research Libraries Information Network). We could search for book titles, conference proceedings, government documents, and much more, not only by author or title, but by subject as well. Once found, the item could be obtained through inter-library loan from the libraries listed as having it.

We also acquired terminals and the necessary staff training to do on-line searching of bibliographic databases through such providers as Lockheed DIALOG, SDC Search Service, National Library of Medicine (MEDLINE and TOXLINE), the New York Times Information Bank, Bibliographic Retrieval Services, and others. All of these services required further equipment.

When I first wanted to show the Caltech professors what we could do for them through such bibliographic searches, I requested a modest sum for a six-month demonstration project. After being turned down for this, I decided to get the money, one way or another. One opportunity came through excess insurance money. Also, we received $6,500 as royalty payments through an agreement with a publisher who used Caltech's file of NACA (National Advisory Committee for Aeronautics) publications to create a marketable microfiche set. We established a Friends of Caltech Libraries support group. We started annual book sales of excess and donated books. Through such means we raised the money to begin acquiring these new on-line services and equipment. By the time I retired in 1981 we had quite a selection of computer equipment.

The professors and students had been won over to the on-line services the library could provide, even if they had to pay the actual costs out of their research budgets. In the year 1980/81 the library staff conducted 892 on-line searches.

While bringing modern technology into the library, we did not neglect other aspects. In 1968 Caltech had started a small program to obtain, index, and retain archives relating to Caltech's history. A highly qualified archivist, Dr. Judith Goodstein, was hired. However, the Institute apparently was not aware of how valuable and necessary an expanded and well-run Archives program could be to such a famous institution. At one time I was told to let the archivist go and hire a part-time clerk to handle whatever had to be done. Both Dr. Goodstein and I bristled at the suggestion. We decided to go after grants and other funds to support the Archives. Dr. Goodstein was able to obtain grants, including one from the National Endowment of the Humanities. One of the items in the Archives was a photograph of Dr. Albert Einstein riding a bicycle in front of a Spanish-style building. Dr. Einstein spent several years at Caltech in the early 1930's. This photograph was enlarged and made into a poster. Dr. Goodstein arranged for its sale through the Smithsonian Institution Gift Shop and other places. The popular demand for this poster brought in thousands of dollars over the years, along with the sale of note cards with illustrations from the rare books collection and other posters.

Dr. Goodstein also established an Oral History Program for recording Caltech's history through the memories of its distinguished older faculty and administrators. As with other such new programs, the initial phase was funded through private donations rather than through budgetary allocations. These oral history stories have provided a unique source of information, and articles based on them have been published. The Archives has managed to establish a firm footing with the Institute administration.

The Rare Books Room is a small room with some unusual rare scientific publications, but it needed updating in security and equipment. We provided a fire extinguishing system, using halon gas, since water would be ruinous. A burglar alarm system was also installed. Bookcases were provided with locked glass fronts, as an additional measure of security. But we discovered that the glass apparently allowed heat to be trapped, affecting the rare bindings. One-inch holes were drilled through the shelves, so that air could circulate. Our honorary curator, Dr. Alexander Pogo, came in once a week and set a pan of water on the floor to provide the humidity needed.

One day, while taking inventory of the collection, an employee noticed some chewed book spines and what appeared to be mouse droppings on the shelves. We surmised that, while Dr. Pogo left the door open to get the water, a mouse (perhaps an escapee from a nearby biology laboratory?) had dashed in and gone through the holes in the shelves. A carpenter installed wire mesh over the holes to keep out future adventurous mice. In taking inventory of the books, the staff made a photocopy of the title page of each rare book for insurance purposes. All of the books were accounted for!

By the later 1960's photocopying (in lieu of copying by hand or by expensive photographs) made it much easier for someone to make many copies. Publishers feared the loss of sales of books and journals, and pressured Congress to make changes in the Copyright Law, which had not been revised extensively since 1909. Academic libraries thought that copying for research purposes should not trigger royalty fees to publishers.

I became seriously interested in this matter soon after I began to work at Caltech. A photocopy facility in the library was busy all day making copies of articles for professors who did not want to track down the location of publications in the dozens of campus libraries. They sent in request forms for the articles they wanted. Then a library staff member ascertained the location of each item, retrieved it and brought it to the photocopy facility. There it was copied and then sent to the requester.

Would such copying violate the proposed law? I began to read up on the pros and cons. As early as 1973 I participated in a debate during the annual meeting of the American Society for Information Sciences held in Los Angeles. The debate was somewhat limited in scope, but did concern some of the fundamental issues (see Reference 47).

By 1976 the revised law was ready but so complex that it was difficult to understand. I collected articles, wrote to copyright law authorities, and gradually acquired a file drawer full of material on the subject. My interpretation of the law came into focus. In May 1977 I presented a paper at the Institute of Electrical and Electronics Engineers IEEE Conference on Scientific Journals, held in Reston, Virginia. My topic was "Implications of the New Copyright Law for Librarians and Library Users" (see Reference 56).

The law was to go into effect on January 1, 1978. We
displayed prominently on all our copying machines the wording required to warn users about copyright infringement. We
revised our journal copy request form to include the prescribed wording and signature to insure that the requester
was aware of the copyright restrictions. Finally, I requested the Institute's legal department to issue a statement to all
faculty members regarding the copyright law and its effect
on the faculty and the library.

When I didn't hear from them, I called and said,
"Where's the copyright statement? We must get something
out."

"Why don't you write it?" the man replied. "You
know what to say."

I wrote as clear a statement as I could because I
wanted the library to be "off the hook" in case any faculty
member was caught violating the law. I felt I had done my
best to alert everyone.

As time went by we encountered only a few problems.
We would not allow multiple copies of articles to be made
nor a copy of a whole book or major section without obtaining
approval of the copyright owner. We did continue to make
single copies of articles on request on the basis of private
study, scholarship and research, as provided by the law.
We carefully followed all provisions with regard to interlibrary loan photocopies (see References 59 and 63).

Conferences, congresses, symposia and similar as-
semblies generate proceedings which are a major class of
scientific and technical literature. Scientists travel world-
wide and exchange information at such meetings. Although
conferences were held as long ago as the seventeenth century,
a tremendous spurt in such meetings began in the 1950's and
has continued unabated.

Such proceedings appear as individual books and as
parts of journals. To cope with this literature there are
many indexes and lists. One problem is that many such
lists appear many months after the original publication of
the proceedings. In order to provide Caltech scientists with
immediate access to this valuable resource, I initiated our
own index of proceedings appearing in current journals received by Caltech libraries.

From August 1976 through October 1981 (the end of my last fiscal year at Caltech) the library cataloged 3,888 such proceedings by subject and sponsoring agencies of these conferences. Also indexed are special topical issues of journals. The index cards are prepared and filed within a few days of receipt of the journals. Once a month a list of these items received during the month is distributed to branch librarians on campus to alert them and their faculty clientele to this important information. At the present time more than fifty conference proceedings and eighty special subject issues are indexed monthly. To my knowledge no other academic library provides such a service.

The preceding examples illustrate some of the challenges I faced as an administrator of a small academic library system, and some of the solutions which I activated. My eight years at Caltech were professionally stimulating and personally rewarding. I had endeavored to bring fruitful results and long-lasting values to the Institute and its libraries. After over forty-four years as a career librarian I could finally retire from full-time employment.

PART II:

TALES OF A LIBRARIAN

WHAT'S MY LINE?

Let's try a game of word association. What profession do you think of when you read or hear "ambulance chaser," "take two," "slide rule," "pork barrel," "open wide," "shhh"? You probably think immediately of lawyer, doctor, engineer, politician, dentist, librarian. You are reacting to common stereotypes, even though these professional people perform important tasks. My line happens to be science/technical information specialist and library administrator, but you'd call me a librarian.

The stereotype of the librarian has been around for a long time. Back in 1939 someone wrote a letter to the "Voice of the People" section of the then lively Los Angeles Daily News:

> Take these librarians. Except for a few higher executives, they have a sinecure, doing little but checking cards and a small amount of filing. They enjoy good hours. They feel secure in a steady position.... Let all salaries of government [employees] in our county and the city of Los Angeles be at least two-thirds reduced.... Were this done, how the crafty politicians would flee -- and I do mean flea.

At that time I was working a forty-four-hour week, earning $115 a month. I was mad!!! Not only were librarians accused of merely checking and filing cards, but

they were thrown in with "crafty politicians"! I sat right
down and wrote a reply in defense of members of my profession. After describing the special training required, the
full-time and odd hours of work and the small pay, I continued:

> Librarianship is as much a profession as teaching,
> practicing law or medicine.... If librarianship con-
> sists merely of "filing a few cards," then who will
> be able to select the comparatively few books a
> library buys from the thousands published; know
> where and how to buy [them]; classify the books...;
> prepare and arrange the detailed catalog cards...;
> compile a variety of reading lists and advise hun-
> dreds of readers...; know what statistics to keep...;
> know how to prepare and stay within a limited budget,
> providing a maximum of public service at minimum
> cost?
>
> Surely it takes trained and capable persons to
> carry out all these specialized duties. Although
> the average public sees only the clerical handling
> of books at a charge desk, there is a great deal
> of professional work done behind the scenes, of
> which the above outline is merely an indication.
> Does W.W. still consider library work an easy and
> political sugar plum?

Some forty years later my ire was roused once more
by an advertisement in the California State Bar Journal (v.
53, no. 4, p. 229, July/August 1978), placed by the Association of California State Attorneys. It showed a photograph
of a female, complete with hair in a bun, wire-rimmed
glasses perched on her nose, in the process of shelving
books. The ad said: "What do attorneys and librarians have
in common? Nothing! So why should state attorneys be
lumped in a collective bargaining group with librarians? Or
rodent and weed inspectors, traffic engineers, maintenance
personnel and other non-professionals?"

Come now! Librarians probably wouldn't want to be
in the same collective bargaining unit with lawyers either,
but do we take out ads depicting lawyers as money-grabbing,
ambulance chasing, selfish creatures ready to sue you for the
slightest excuse? I wrote as much to the editor and continued:

> You and your peers know that the majority of law-
> yers are especially trained, hard working and often

compassionate professionals, and some no doubt
have grey hair, glasses and toupees. So why malign
another profession through time-worn, outdated
stereotypes?

When you go to a law library do you see grey-
ing female librarians with buns? More likely you'll
find a male professional with legal as well as
library science training. When a doctor goes to
a medical library he needs specialists, men and
women, trained in the latest computerized information retrieval methods to help find what he needs
in the voluminous literature. Librarians these days
must be familiar with a variety of computerized
cataloging and bibliographic searching techniques.
It is the library clerks or aides who do the shelving, not the professional librarians.

Just as a lawyer is an expert in laws, legal
citations and precedents, a librarian is an expert
in bibliographic know-how -- what is published, how
to acquire and catalog it for effective retrieval,
how to identify incomplete and inaccurate references,
how to find any information requested, or how to
find out what a user really wants. Many librarians
write, give lectures, do research, attend and participate in professional organization meetings, teach,
provide specialized skills, and do all the things that
other professionals do. Their education now requires six years of college, two of which are in post-
graduate library science schools, and the courses
are quite demanding. Many librarians become competent administrators, dealing with personnel management, budget preparation and control, architectural
and space planning and similar involved tasks.

Letters from persons who had seen the ad before I did were
published in the November/December 1978 issue. Diane C.H.
Reynolds, Head Reference Librarian, Los Angeles County
Law Library and Member of the California State Bar wrote:

> ... I believe a properly trained law librarian is an
> indispensable resource that the legal community
> should begin to acknowledge and must learn to
> rely upon in order to meet the needs of prospective
> clients.... Unfortunately the question, answer, and
> picture displayed in the advertisement allows a
> particular attitude and stereotype of librarians to
> be re-emphasized in the minds of persons who read

our professional literature. Most librarians con-
tinuously fight such an undeserved image and they
should expect the <u>Journal</u> to help them destroy, not
propagate, this undeserved image....

Sharon S. Peterson, another law librarian, wrote:

... As a law librarian, I resent being grouped with
rodent and weed inspectors and being called "nonprofessional." As a woman, I resent the implication
that female librarians are mere book shelvers....
For your information, law is not the only profession.... Managing the many systems in a library,
supervising personnel, maintaining control over
burgeoning publications and retrieving materials
quickly are professional tasks that I found most attorneys do not even begin to comprehend.... The
point could have been made just as adequately without taking pot-shots at a profession that is just as
viable as law and, because of the honesty within
its ranks, much more credible to the public at
large. The advertiser owes an apology to librarians
specifically and women in general. As a future attorney, I am very embarrassed by these advertising tactics.

J. Myron Jacobstein, President, American Association
of Law Libraries, Director of Stanford University Law Library and Professor of Law wrote:

... I indeed find it shocking that your journal would
carry an advertisement which so calumniously at-
tacks a related profession, especially when such an
advertisement is in spirit, if not in actuality, in
violation of the California Business and Professional
Code.... I do hope you will see fit to place in a
prominent place an apology to the library profession
in the next issue of your journal.

Frank Evans, president of the Association of California State Attorneys, which had placed the advertisement,
finally offered an apology.

Please accept my sincere apology. It was not our
intent to offend any profession, and I regret that
the ad conveyed this impression.... We are at-
tempting to form a collective bargaining unit com-

posed exclusively of attorneys.... We prefer our
own unit for several important reasons. Our pref-
erence is, however, not based on a feeling of
superior status, and it is not our intent to disparage
any trade, craft or profession.

In order to convey our message, we retained
"R" Agency, a public relations firm, which prepared the ad that I approved. I did not, and do not
now, think the ad offensive.... I do think that
it is eye-catching and accomplishes our first ob-
jective.... I felt that the message would convey
the intent of the Association and explain any miscon-
ceptions that might arise. Finally, I wish to state
that the Association and all attorneys hold librarians
in high esteem, and it is important to acknowledge
the valuable services that they render lawyers and
the public. *

If the intent was to indicate his organization's pref-
erence for its own collective bargaining unit, why mention
librarians as nonprofessional, and lump them with other
occupations which they obviously considered beneath themselves?

Part of the problem is that the tag "librarian" is so
definitely linked with books (Latin "liber"). Yet librarians
deal with a great variety of materials--periodicals, documents, manuscripts, maps, music scores, records, slides,
patents, etc. What is needed are new words for people who
work professionally in this environment.

Years ago the head librarian of a Navy library was
having trouble getting higher pay for his librarians who were
designated as order librarians, reference librarians, and
catalogers. When he tried to get them upgraded, he was
told that "ordering" was a clerk's job, the reference librarian
"just referred" to some reference books, and the cataloger
probably "prepared a catalog, " whatever that is.

The head librarian then devised some titles which
would have more of a Navy ring. He wrote up new job descriptions for a "procurement officer" and "information
specialist. " I don't recall what he tagged the cataloger, but

---

* Letters reprinted with permission of <u>California Lawyer</u>,
successor to the <u>California State Bar Journal.</u>

let's say it was "bibliographic analyst." Well! If these
people are officers and specialists and analysts, then they
obviously aren't clerks. So the reclassifications, with higher
salaries, were approved.

Having worked as a technical and engineering librarian
for over forty years I feel qualified to describe what an engineering librarian is and does. A professional librarian
knows how to order all kinds of publications (documents, technical reports, journals, standards, etc.) from a variety of
sources; to index and classify them according to established
and proven procedures for best arrangement and retrieval
as needed; to find published and unpublished information in
unusual places; to plan the layout and equipment for the specific needs of the library; to interface with library users in
order to ascertain what they need in the way of reference
resources; to prepare and manage a budget; and to handle
personnel.

From time to time a job announcement for an engineering librarian specifies that the applicant must have both an
engineering and a library science degree. Why? Nowhere
is there a requirement that the engineering librarian design
a highway or bridge, or perform some other engineering
function. Obviously the librarian can become sufficiently
familiar with specialized terminology to do the indexing or
reference work required. He/she does not need to understand every article and book in the library.

There are actually a few engineers who also obtain
the library science degree and vice versa. They are, of
course, well qualified. But, if the employer must choose
someone with only the one degree, do not hire an engineer
without library training. I have known a number of these,
but they were nearly always failures, with a few bright
exceptions. Their engineering know-how is of limited value
in their role as librarians. Without training in library
science, they cannot do the work involved.

When the Armed Services Technical Information Agency
(ASTIA) was first established to index thousands of technical
reports, their management did not want the advice of librarians who were considered as old-fashioned shy creatures.
Instead, young engineers and scientists were hired who might
understand the subject content of the reports but who knew
nothing of the proper indexing techniques or how literature is
searched and located in libraries. It wasn't long before their

failures became obvious, and soon professional librarians
were called on for their expertise to do the indexing properly.

In the late 1950's I began to teach a class on the literature of science and engineering, as an extension course aimed
at engineers. The first class consisted of two engineers and
nine librarians from industrial libraries. At the end of the
course one of the engineers said to me: "I learned a lot
from this course. I learned that the literature is too complex for me to bother learning. All I need to get the information is to ask the right librarian!" The librarians all
said: "We're the ones the engineers turn to when they want
information. So we need to know all about the technical literature." Most engineers just don't want to bother to learn
the intricacies of coping with the vast amount of technical
literature. The course then became part of the curriculum
in the UCLA Graduate School of Library Service, enabling
library school students to become proficient in this specialty.

Librarians have tried different terms to designate what
they do: "bibliographer," " documentalist," "library system
analyst," "technical services coordinator," "bibliographic
data researcher," "technical information specialist," "information officer," "data base searcher," and similar phrases.
But generally librarians are still called "librarians." They
are professionals involved with bibliographic services. They
don't charge out books, nor shelve them, nor say "shhhhh"
--and a lot the them are men!

FROG NURSE, DAZZLE PAINTING AND GOLD

The Los Angeles County Public Library is a large
library system providing library services to those county areas
which do not have local municipal libraries. At the time I
worked there as a technical reference librarian (1939-1942),
any question which could not be answered readily in a branch
library was sent to the Central Library, where a staff of reference librarians would research it, find the appropriate
journal, book, document or fact, and send it to the requester.
The only information the reference librarians had about the
request were the few words a library patron wrote on a 3" x
5" slip. There was no opportunity to interrogate the patron
to find out what was really wanted. We did not even know
whether the requester was a child or an adult.

Often the questions were so vague that we couldn't figure out what was really wanted.   One request read "Electric
towels."   I found information on hot air dryers, which are
sometimes used in place of paper towel dispensers.   Within
a short time the request came back with a note from the
branch librarian: "Patron meant electric tools!"

Another question that really stumped me was a brief
request: "Frog nurse."   Now what could that mean?   Is
that a beginning nurse in training, maybe a "frosh nurse"?
I didn't want to guess, so I wrote back for more information.
This time I received a longer note from the branch librarian:
"This is for a young boy who has a sick polliwog and he wants
to know how to make it better."

Many requests were interesting to work on.   "How do
you milk a snake of its venom?"   "Do you have a recipe for
tutti-frutti ice cream?"   "I want to build a smokehouse to
smoke fish."   "What is the fastest elevator in the world?"
"What plant do you grow that, when you burn the roots, you
get gold in the ashes?"   That sounded peculiar, but I found
that there really was such a plant growing on the banks of
the Danube.   The gold, which was in the soil, was absorbed
into the roots by a kind of osmosis.

Just before World War II the country was preparing for
national defense by expanding ship and aircraft production.
Since Los Angeles County was a key area for such activity,
many requests were received in the library for material on
such subjects as blueprint reading, mechanical drawing, metal
working, marine engineering, jigs and machine tools, shipbuilding and airplane design and construction.   There was
also a rush for aircraft identification manuals.

When we received many requests for information on
blackouts for home and camouflage for industries, we found
that during World War I battleships were painted with zigzag
stripes called dazzle painting, which, it was hoped, would
make the ships disappear as an optical illusion.   I still remember seeing the Douglas Aircraft Company plant in Santa
Monica painted to look like houses, with window curtains and
laundry on the lines.

Through finding answers to such a variety of questions
I learned about many interesting things, such as the meaning
of tree rings; abalone shells and the culture of pearls; vegetable stains and colors discovered and used by American

Indians; turkey raising in California; formulas for different
kinds of glass; orchid culture; recipe for Irish potato bread;
culture of water chestnuts; description of various breeds of
American saddle horses; handmade candles; building plans
for small chicken house; raising mink.

All of this was wonderful training for a librarian. You
could not tell the patron to "look in that index," since the
patron was not there. The librarian had to do all the searching, locate the best article, chapter, document, technical
report or pamphlet, utilizing a great many abstracting and
indexing tools and reference books. The material was sent
to the lucky reader in his/her branch library.

This exposure to scientific and technical questions and
the finding of suitable answers started me on my subsequent
long career as a science/technical literature specialist.

THE RAZOR'S EDGE AND I

B.T. (before television) the movie studios took great
pains to make everything in a picture authentic. The Research Departments (that's what they called their libraries)
were stocked with Sears, Roebuck and Montgomery Ward
catalogs going back many years, so that all styles of clothes
and types of equipment would be according to the time setting
of the story. Lady Godey's books on fashion from the nineteenth century were carefully preserved. Thousands of magazine and newspaper clippings were kept, all organized by subject. Anything pictorial was noted and indexed.

As an example of the attention given to detail the
Metro-Goldwyn-Mayer Studios Research Department maintained
a complete file of automobile license plate information --
the colors, letters, numbers, slogans, size, etc. -- for
every category of car in every state since license plates
were first issued in the United States. Suppose the film
depicted a truck driving through Iowa in 1928. The file
would show just how a commercial license plate should look
to match that place and time. Why? Well, perhaps someone in Iowa who had kept such a license plate tacked up in
his garage for many years would let the studio know in no
uncertain terms if the prop department had goofed.

When the studio librarians couldn't find the reference

they needed, they would call up the local libraries for help.
One day, when I was working at the Reference Desk at the
UCLA Library, I had a call from the Twentieth Century-Fox
Research Department. They were filming The Razor's Edge,
starring Tyrone Power. The producer was looking for a book
in Sanskrit on philosophy. In one of the film's scenes the
high priest (played by the late Sam Jaffe), would be reading
this high in the Himalayas, when Tyrone would arrive, seek-
ing spiritual guidance.

First I found out what Sanskrit looked like. Then I
checked for suitable books in the card catalog and book stacks.
I located a book in Sanskrit on literature and reasoned: "Hin-
du literature and philosophy are almost synonymous. This
should do." But when I called the studio librarian, she said
no, it must be on philosophy, not literature. After all, some
Sanskrit scholar watching the film would see that it was literature and not philosophy. Finally I found a publication from
the University of Madras which (from bibliographical evidence
in English) appeared to be on philosophy, and it was in Sanskrit!
The paperbound book appeared rather drab but the librarian
was happy when I told her I had found what they were looking for. The studio quickly sent someone to pick it up.

For further authenticity and beauty, the studio had
some of the text copied on vellum and the finished pages
bound in a sumptuous beautiful leather binding. The impressive scene was shot. But -- alas! In the editing it ended
up on the cutting room floor. When I learned about this and
commiserated with the studio librarian about all our work
for naught, she said: "Think nothing of it. We're used to
it because it happens all the time." Librarians in all the
studio libraries loved their work. There was never a job
vacancy as these librarians stayed until they retired.

When Universal Studios made The Egg and I, the
Publicity Department came up with a clever idea for the
premiere. What if everyone there received a hard-boiled
egg which, when peeled, would have the inscription THE
EGG AND I visible on the solid egg white? The Research
Department was asked to look into this.

The studio librarian went to the Magic Shop on Hollywood Boulevard and explained her mission. The attendant
said: "Yes, we have such a fluid. You write on the shell
of the hard boiled egg, and the writing will be invisible. But
when you peel the egg, the writing becomes visible on the

egg white." The librarian took some of the magic fluid and tried it out at home. It worked! So she reported the success of her mission to the Publicity Department.

Eventually someone had second thoughts: "What are we going to do with all the egg shells on the floor of the theater?"

WHAT'S WRONG WITH YOUR LIBRARY?

When I visited a number of engineering libraries in 1946, I usually asked the librarian: "If you could start this library over again, or make changes, what would you do differently?" This was a polite way of asking: "What's wrong with your library?" And there were many illuminating answers.

One of the institutions had built a new building, including the library, as soon as the war ended. One of our professors, who had gone on a trip to visit engineering schools and buildings, said: "You must go and see this library. It's beautiful and large!"

As I walked in I thought I had entered a church. At the far end, about ninety feet away, was a counter which looked like an altar. Behind it was the portrait of the donor, hung against beautiful drapes. Large reading tables throughout the room reminded me of pews. Shelves of reference books lined the walls, making it difficult for a reference librarian to do quick reference work from a desk. Near the counter was the card catalog. On either side of the counter were two small offices. If the librarian wanted to speak to the assistant, he had to cross behind the counter. To return a book one had to walk the ninety feet to the counter and then all the way back -- a 180-foot stretch!

Passing through the door behind the counter one entered a long, rather narrow area. One side was lined with study cubicles. "Sit down," the librarian said, "and pretend to be studying." As soon as I bent my head, it cast a shadow on the reading area because the light was centered in the middle of the cubicle rather than over the reading matter.

The rest of the space was taken up by short ranges of book stacks. There were two levels of stacks. Was there

Beautiful but impractical for a busy technical library.

an elevator for people and/or book trucks? No, there was only a small book lift. You put a few books on the lift, press a button, then walk up. A book truck was permanently stationed on the second floor. You take the books out of the book list and then put them on the truck for shelving.

There were so many bad features about this library that one librarian had already quit. As a result of this visit I made sure that my library would have the following:

1. The circulation counter right by the entrance/exit.

2. Offices arranged for better communication.

3. Cubicles with proper lights.

4. A full elevator for both people and book trucks.

5. A reference collection concentrated in one area, not dispersed along the walls of a large room.

Another interesting library, in a well-known institute of technology, was housed in a round building. The center was a large reference room, with balconies on upper floors. Between the reference room and the outside wall were offices, such as the Cataloging Department. The card catalog was built right into the wall separating the two departments, so the drawers could be pulled out from either side. "How ingenious, " I thought. In the Cataloging Department I noticed that the drawers had latches on them. When I asked what they were for, my guide said: "Well, the students used to give the drawers a strong push, and the drawers would come sailing out here. So we had to put these stops on them."

I also visited the Architecture branch library at this institution. When I asked my standard question, the librarian could hardly wait to tell me what she would do differently.

"Don't get black Kardexes!" (Note: A Kardex [trade name] file has flat drawers containing pockets to hold cards with information on periodical volumes and issues. These are extremely useful, but in recent times many libraries have converted their records to computer files. For more on serial records in Kardex files, see Reference 11.)

"What's wrong with black Kardexes?" I asked. "They look beautiful with the matte finish and chromium trim."

"Look what happens, " she answered, and pulled out a drawer. I saw that the cards immediately curled. "It's the heat drawn in by the black finish. If I were you, I'd get a lighter color."

Another note for my notebook. Subsequently I ordered light gray files for my library.

"See those air conditioning vents on the floor?" she continued. "Don't ever get them. The janitors push dust in them. When they get clogged the air has no place to go. The air pushes open the doors and we can't close them. Then we have to call and have someone come to clean out the vents. So get them on the walls or ceilings."

At another university I picked up a useful tip. In answer to my question the branch librarian said: "I would get light switches near the exit door. When the library is being closed for the night you can turn off all the lights at one place. We have to go to each stack range and turn off

individual lights.   That takes a lot of time when you're closing up. "

When I returned to UCLA I had a notebook full of
ideas, many of which were subsequently incorporated in the
final Engineering Library space into which we moved in 1959.
One of the best ideas was to install a public address system
throughout the three stack levels and the reading room.   In
talking to the architects I asked them to install such a system.
When we were ready to move in, I didn't see the microphone
and equipment, and asked the architect about it.   "Oh, we
put the piping and outlets in, just where you want them.
But the equipment -- speakers and microphone -- you have
to order separately."   NOW he tells me!   There was no
money set aside for this equipment.   It was six months before the equipment was finally installed.

We were delighted.   We could now announce closing
time, instead of scaring people half to death by switching lights
on and off.   We could call a reference librarian who was in
the stacks, or call a library user who had a reserve book
overdue, when other users were asking for it.   And we would
occasionally be able to page a reader in an emergency.

The most dramatic use was the day President Kennedy
was shot.   I happened to be in the Geology Library when a
secretary dashed in with the unbelievable news.   Immediately
I returned to the Engineering Building.   A friend in the hall
said that the Dean had a TV in his office.   We went in to
learn the shooting details.   When it was announced that the
President had died, I went back to the Engineering Library
and asked a student assistant to make the announcement on
the public address system.   I just couldn't speak.   The students came pouring out of the stacks and reading room trying to find a nearby radio or TV.

Working with the architects on the library plans, I
learned several useful things.   First, some architects apparently do not learn how to design libraries in architecture
school.   They don't know the flow of materials and people
in a library, and the relationship of card catalog, circulation
desk, a reference area, book stacks and offices.   Second,
besides looking at floor plans, the librarian should consider
what is to go on columns and walls.   I had planned some
shelving to abut a column, when I learned that the architects
had attached a thermostat on that side of the column.   Another
column had a fire-extinguisher where it would be in the way

of shelving. Finally, find out how the ceiling lighting will
go with your shelving. It may turn out that the lights will
shine down on top of your shelves, instead of down the middle
of the aisles. A solution is to have the lights go cross-wise
to the stacks, so there will always be lights in the aisles.

So when you learn what's wrong with someone else's
library, you can do what's right for yours.

THE TAIL THAT WAGGED THE DOG

How do you find a book in a library? Look in the
card catalog, of course. But what if the word you look under
doesn't show the book? Does that mean the library doesn't
have it? Not necessarily. It may be listed under another
term and no cross-reference was made. The book may be
"brief-listed" under the author only. There are more reasons.
A catalog is only as good as the cataloger makes it.

As the first professional librarian in charge of a branch
library at UCLA, I was determined that there be a complete
card catalog in the Engineering Library, with entries under
authors, various forms of the titles, contemporary subjects
and adequate cross-references, plus other useful information.
Since the catalog would be started "from scratch" I wanted to
avoid all of the pitfalls of existing catalogs where the excuse
was this: "It costs too much to change."

At that time, many libraries, including UCLA, used
Library of Congress catalog cards because they were complete,
presumably accurate and easy to obtain. (One of the things I
learned in library school was that the Library of Congress
catalogers could sometimes make an error. In cataloging
class I found something on an L.C. card that I could not
understand. When I asked the professor to explain it, she
said: "Oh, L.C. goofed. That is obviously wrong." My
idol of L.C. as the god of cataloging was forever shattered.)

Soon it became evident that the L.C. subject headings
for technical subjects were considerably behind modern times.
For example, the British spelling of "aeroplanes" was adopted
by L.C. early in the century. Long before 1945 American
usage became "airplanes," and I was not about to go back
to the British version. Nor was I willing to have books on
ceramic engineering, a new technical field, listed under the

L. C. heading of "Pottery." Another problem was the term
for computers, which were just coming into prominence.
The UCLA College of Engineering was planning on going
strongly into this new field, and we were purchasing the
latest publications. What was the term L. C. used for these?
"Calculating machines." Although this is technically correct,
that phrase was already being limited to desk-top electric adding machines. No one was calling huge computers (they were
huge at that time), a "calculating machine." So we began
to use not only "Computers," but also its developing branches
of "Computers, Analog" and "Computers, Digital." There
were many other examples of headings which I felt the Catalog Department should change to make our catalog match the
contemporary usage.

Another matter was the description of special features
of a book. Cataloging rules specify that such extra features
as illustrations, plates, maps, and tables be listed on catalog
cards, but such notations should be used with discretion. I
noticed that the Catalog Department was diligently searching
through all of our newly acquired books to see if they contained "tables," i.e. mathematical data in tabular form. If
the cataloger found just one table in a book, she would add
the information to the card, even if L. C. had not included
it. But since nearly all engineering books contain tables,
adding that information on the cards just isn't necessary.
When I talked to the cataloger about this, I said: "We expect
to find tables in technical books. It would be more useful
if you omitted that but noted any technical book that does not
have tables. Just say 'no tables'." She laughed slightly and
replied: "But I couldn't do that. That's not in the rules."

There was something the Catalog Department wanted
to omit from typed cards, the size of the book. Normally
the size is given in centimeters. As soon as I heard of this,
I said: "Now wait a minute! That is important information.
It supplies the second dimension of a book, the first being
the number of pages. If I'm looking for a book on the shelf,
it helps to know if it is thick and normal height (350 pages
and 23 cm.), narrow and tall (50 pages and 28 cm.), or even
narrow and small (40 pages and 18 cm.). So please leave in
the size on the catalog card."

Following a few more such disagreements, someone
in the Catalog Department said to me: "You're just like the
tail that wagged the dog. We can't make all these changes
just to please you! We have to follow our normal procedures."

After a while we reached a truce. The Catalog Department would do all of the cataloging except the subject headings. In the Engineering Library catalog I could add any heading I wanted, while they could continue to use what they wanted on their cards for the main University Library Catalog -- "Aeroplanes, " "calculating machines, " "pottery" and all the rest.

We sent a list of the headings we preferred to the Library of Congress. After a number of years they finally did change many of such outmoded headings, even though this was a considerable expense because of their vast catalogs. But many libraries found the expense too great and kept the old headings.

Unfortunately, there were other problems, notably the length of time it took to catalog our books. Here we were building a library from the ground up and needed the books we ordered. Technical books go out of date quickly and waiting six months to a year for our books through the ordering and cataloging process was just too long. Finally the accumulated backlog proved too much, and I alerted the College of Engineering Faculty Library Committee. (Sometimes it is expedient to use a little extra clout.) Its investigation brought pressure to bear with the library administration. In July 1953 the complete cataloging process was transferred to the Engineering Library, with an allocation for a staff cataloger and one typist clerk. At last we were in control of our catalog destiny! (See Reference 16 in the Bibliography.)

In 1965 the cataloging for the other physical sciences libraries -- Chemistry, Geology/Geophysics and Physics -- was also transferred to us. We were no longer the tail, but the top dog!

SPRECHEN SIE DEUTSCH?

Soon after Wernher von Braun, the German missile expert, was captured by the Americans in 1945, he and about forty other scientists in his group were brought to White Sands Proving Grounds in New Mexico. There they began to work on the United States guided missile program.

By 1949 the government decided that these scientists could no longer be kept in technical military custody. They

began their official status as immigrants and were allowed to
travel. Two of them came to the School of Engineering at
UCLA to give some lectures. When the government released
the men entirely to go wherever they pleased, these two were
asked to become professors.

One of them was Dr. Heinz Haber, a well-known phys-
icist. He was rather shy, but he opened up when I spoke
to him in my native German. One day he came to the library and said to me: "I wonder if you could help me find
this German journal which I need for my research. When
I was at White Sands no one was able to identify or locate
it. " I took one look at his reference and recognized the ab-
breviated citation as a journal which we had. I walked down
the aisle, pulled it off the shelf and handed it to him. He
clasped the book to his breast and exclaimed: "To think I
have been under the same roof with this book for six weeks!"
Obviously he was so pleased that I, too, felt a glow of sat-
isfaction in having been able to be of service.

Sometime later I had a call from the librarian at the
Walt Disney Studios. Did I know an engineer who spoke
German? They wanted to put in a transatlantic telephone call
to Germany to discuss some matter with a German engineer.
Right away I thought of Dr. Haber and asked him if he would
be interested. He was pleased to carry out the assignment.
In fact, he so impressed the Disney people that he became the
full-time chief science consultant to the Studio. One of the
Disney pictures he worked on was Man in Space. This ani-
mated film showed the effect of weightlessness and other problems which would be faced in space flight. This helped prepare the public to understand the subsequent flights by our
astronauts.

During this time preparations were being made for the
opening of Disneyland. Walt Disney asked Dr. Haber if he
could somehow demonstrate the principle of nuclear fission,
so that the general public could comprehend how it worked.
This was not to be anything elaborate, just effective. The
opening ceremonies were a highlight of the television season.
When the moment came for the nuclear fission simulation, the
camera zoomed in on a hundred (a thousand?) mousetraps,
each set with a pingpong ball. At the critical moment, Dr.
Haber's son threw in one ball. In a split second a white
cloud of balls exploded as balls and mousetraps set off each
other. It was a hilarious as well as impressive spectacle.

Dr. Haber became so interested in the use of television to promote scientific ideas that he returned to Germany to put on similar TV programs there. Later he became publisher and chief editor of a German scientific journal, Bild der Wissenschaft, somewhat akin to Scientific American.

SPUTNIK AND MAN IN SPACE

On October 4, 1957, Sputnik I, the first man-made satellite, was launched by the Soviet Union. This orbit of the earth opened a new space exploration age. The event surprised the rest of the world. Why didn't anyone in our country know about it in advance? Someone told me that the radio frequency of Sputnik had been published in the August issue of a Russian radio amateur magazine. A quick check of our files showed we had that issue, but apparently no reader had spotted that article.

There's nothing like a world event to get a little publicity for one's favorite subject. Sputnik had captured the public's interest in technical matters. On December 6 the Santa Monica Evening Outlook, in its regular column "The Professor Speaks," printed an article I had submitted, adding a sub-title "... On Information, Please!"

When you see or read about new technological marvels, such as solar batteries on the "USAtellite," electric lighting from atomic power stations, anti-missile missiles, or ERMA the banking computer, do you sometimes wonder just where the research scientists and engineers get all the information needed to develop and produce these intricate machines and mechanisms?

Experimentation through trial and error is certainly part of the answer, but a great deal of information is accumulated by reading many journals, books and reports pertinent to the research project.

There is no lack of written information on all kinds of subjects. It is estimated that two million articles and books on scientific and technical subjects are published each year. It would take a single reader more than one hundred years just to read all of the scientific literature published in one year.

The research man is confronted with two basic problems in regard to this vast pool of scientific

and technical literature: (1)   How can he find out
what has been written on his particular subject?
And (2)   Where can he find the publication, once
he knows the specific reference he needs?   In both
of these problems he can turn to a specialist in
bibliographic matters, a qualified librarian.

The larger industrial and research laboratories
maintain special libraries to serve the needs of
their research staffs.   Professional experienced librarians, familiar with the indexes, reference books,
and the know-how of finding specific information,
are available to help.

Smaller companies often cannot afford to establish and maintain large library collections and hire
qualified librarians.   Even the larger companies
cannot possibly hope to build up completely adequate
collections of all of the journals, books and reports
they will ever need.

The obvious thing to do is to find a really large
library that can supplement the smaller libraries.
The metropolitan public libraries can sometimes
fill the needs, but it is the university libraries,
with their vast research collections and specialized
staffs, that become the hub of such informational
activity as is required for research projects.

The article went on to explain how our Engineering
Library and other special collections on the campus handled
the thousands of requests from many states and foreign countries.

The Sputnik event impelled scientists and engineers
throughout the world to become more interested in Russian
publications in science and technology.   Thanks to Dean
Boelter's early suggestion that the Engineering Library col-
lect Russian journals, we already had one of the best collections in the United States.   As requests from other libraries came pouring in, we stepped up the building of our
Russian collection.   In order to be able to handle material
in Russian I took a year of Russian language, and then taught
my staff to read the Slavic alphabet and recognize, in Russian,
such words as volume, number, and the months of the year,
so that they could check in journal issues properly.

On August 28, 1959, several newspapers announced that
additional Russian scientific material would be available at
UCLA.   According to one article:

UCLA has been named by the U.S. Department of Commerce as one of the four depositories in the U.S. for translated Russian technical journals, it was announced jointly today by Mrs. Johanna E. Tallman, engineering librarian at UCLA, and Edwin Bates, manager of the Commerce Department's Los Angeles field office.

The publications are being supplied by the Commerce Department's Office of Technical Services -- the federal government's clearing house for translations of technical and scientific literature.

... A vast fund of Russian material is being made available to faculty researchers and to Southern California's scientific and industrial community through this depository arrangement.

The article listed the categories of publications which would be available, including semimonthly summaries, prepared by the U.S. Central Intelligence Agency, of technical and scientific articles published in the Sino-Soviet orbit and in Yugoslavia. The three other depositories were the Massachusetts Institute of Technology, the John Crerar Library in Chicago, and the Georgia Institute of Technology.

Another event startled the world on April 12, 1961: "First Man Orbits Earth in Space!" This was Russian cosmonaut Major Yuri Gagarin. Dean Boelter, who was in Germany at the time, brought back a German newspaper item announcing this event.

By now American research was pouring out a tremendous stream of technical reports, a relatively new category of publication. Believing that this was a story of general interest, I prepared information which was released through the University of California Office of Public Information Clip Sheet of November 28, 1961. This story was picked up by various newspapers, including the New York Times (January 14, 1962, Section 4, p. E7). This was the release:

FLOOD OF TECHNICAL REPORTS BRINGS NEW HEADACHES TO LIBRARIES AND INDUSTRY

A flood of technical reports, often equally hard to trace, obtain and classify, has been pouring out of government agencies, universities and industrial laboratories since the end of World War II.

There are now well over a million of these

special publications on engineering and scientific
subjects, and they are increasing at the rate of
100,000 a year, reports Mrs. Johanna Tallman, head
of the UCLA Engineering-Mathematical Sciences Library and lecturer in the School of Library Service.

Rising from this flood is a new type of information specialist, a combination of librarian, scientist-
engineer, and computer expert, who works, index-
in-hand, with scientific teams and usually commands
an impressive salary.

The need for such specialists is recognized by
two groups: (1) Government contractors and other
industries which now frequently duplicate research
which, unknown to them, has been reported elsewhere, and (2) librarians who are faced with a
complex set of new bibliographic headaches.

Some twenty existing and former agencies, from
the Atomic Energy Commission to the Wright Air
Development Center, have been involved in the procurement, indexing and distribution of technical
reports. Their reports come in a bewildering
array of numbering systems, security classifications and methods of reproduction, and range from
brief, poorly-written notes on ephemeral items to
lengthy treatises on vital scientific developments.

Some of the most interesting reports were collected by Allied teams which went into Germany and
Japan at the end of World War II to track down
technical documents and interview scientists and
manufacturers. The Air Force alone screened,
organized and cataloged 1500 tons of Axis documents.

Mrs. Tallman foresees some hope for harassed
librarians in the development of computer techniques
for information retrieval and in the emergence of
centralized distribution offices, such as the Armed
Services Technical Information Agency, which now
handles all technical reports originating with the
Army, Navy and Air Force and their contractors.

But meanwhile, she sees no easy short-cut for
librarians, except to familiarize themselves with
the special jargons and bibliographic complexities
of technical reports.

Libraries had definitely entered the Information Age.

For information on the history and importance of
technical reports, see Reference 26. For anyone interested

in a more complete description of technical reports and their
indexes, the author can offer a 31-page list based on her
lecture on this subject in the UCLA Graduate School of Library Science.

PERILS OF PUBLISHING

High hopes for success ride on a new project.   Surely
your super idea will work out the way you imagine it!   But
developments may bring about unanticipated problems.

In the 1950's it was common practice in special libraries to route new journal issues to members of the research staff.   The last person on the list might not get the
issue until weeks or even months after it was originally received.   In those days, before the advent of photocopying,
some librarians prepared and routed lists of the tables of
contents of the journals instead of the actual issues.   Thus
the journal itself would remain accessible in the library.

Four of us librarians (W. Roy Holleman, Margaret
Whitnah, Sol J. Grossman and I) decided, as an extracurricular activity, to publish monthly the tables of contents from
a selection of current scientific and technical journals.   At
the modest subscription price of $8 per year, a library
could obtain several copies and do away with the bother of
making its own lists.   We called ourselves "Technical Library Associates. "   The publication, entitled Technical
Contents, was launched in January 1958.   We arranged with
the publishers of the journals we had selected to send us
their tables of contents in advance (usually galley proofs).
By the time our subscribers received our publication, the
journals themselves were just arriving.   Thus the information provided by Technical Contents was very current--a
good sales pitch for obtaining subscriptions.   Our first issue
comprised ninety-four pages.   The list of journals expanded
as the demand for this service increased.

In March of 1958 we received a letter from a Philadelphia lawyer, informing us that the Institute for Scientific
Information, located in Philadelphia, had the exclusive right
to the word "Contents" because it had been publishing Current
Contents for the previous six months.   This was also a table
of contents publication, but the journals covered were mostly
on pharmaceutical subjects.   The lawyer said it was like

Reader's Digest pre-empting the word "Digest." Could they
really prevent us from using Technical Contents for our publication?

Jake Zeitlin, a friend and renowned antiquarian book-
seller with useful contacts, recommended an attorney at
Universal Studios. Motion picture studios often had to con-
tend with people who accused them of using their name in a
movie. It seemed to us that using similar names and similar
titles had something in common. Two of us went to see the
attorney. As soon as we explained our problem and he found
out how poor we were, he said: "You can't afford my fee.
But I have an associate who might be willing to give you some
brief advice and write a letter for you."

Although it seemed reasonable to us that we were not
infringing on Current Contents by using Technical Contents,
the second lawyer told us that a lawsuit, especially in Philadelphia, would be very expensive, and there would be no
guarantee that a jury would vote in our favor. He advised
us to give up our title on condition that the Institute could
not use it for their projected Current Contents of Space,
Electronics and Physical Sciences, which would deal with
many of the same journals covered in our publication. He
said: "If you have a product that libraries really need and
want, it doesn't really matter what you call it." We took
his advice, he wrote a letter to the Philadelphia lawyer,
whose client then agreed not to use our title. We proceeded
to look for a new title.

On the cover of the April 1958 issue we unveiled our
changed title:

This is "ITT"

INTERNATIONAL
TECHNICAL
TITLES

In the editorial we explained that it had been necessary to change the title. Since we covered technical journals
from several countries and since we listed titles, not abstracts, we felt that our new title was appropriate. We
added:

Our only concern now with our new title and front
cover design is that they do not cause confusion

through identification with a well-known communications company.

This was written as a bit of humor, but in the next mail--you guessed it!--arrived a letter from a New York lawyer for the huge International Telephone and Telegraph Company, telling us that they had the exclusive right to use "ITT. " We should cease and desist using that or else... ! Now how did a big outfit like that find out about four librarians in Los Angeles publishing an 800-copy list of tables of contents? Well, we didn't need a lawyer this time to advise us. We dropped "This is 'ITT' " with the next issue, but retained our full title.

We had no more trouble with our remaining title, but publishing and maintaining subscriptions was hard work, especially since we did it on our own time. After two years on this endeavor we quit and left the market to our Philadelphia competitor. We did not feel bitter about our legal encounter with Current Contents. In fact, we have remained on friendly terms with the president of the Institute for Scientific Information.

ADVENTURES IN PARTIAL TITLES

At a meeting in 1959 of the Library Council--the chief administrators and the librarians of large library units and branch libraries at UCLA--the cost of cataloging and card catalogs came up. Among the suggestions made was one that we drop what librarians call "partial titles. "

Normally a book is entered in the card catalog under the first word of the title (except an initial article). Occasionally there are books where the first word of the title is insignificant or there are some subsequent words which are more likely to be remembered. In such a case an entry is made under the significant words, and this is called a partial title entry.

As soon as the suggestion was made to drop these, I spoke up. "They're much too important. Sometimes they are the only way to locate a book if you don't know the author. Please keep them in. " The University Librarian, Dr. Powell, suggested that I write out my reasons for the next meeting. As we were leaving, he came up to me and said: "Make it funny!"

How do you make such a dull subject as partial titles
funny? I finally came up with the following piece. The
catalog card used as the title for this article shows three
partial titles under which cards are to be filed. Each of
the titles in the story is real and was in the UCLA Library
catalog at the time. I merely pretended that the partial
titles had not been made, in line with the proposed policy.

As a result of this bit of humor, the Council subsequently decided to retain partial titles in the UCLA Library
catalog. The article itself was published in the Special Libraries Association Southern California Chapter Bulletin (see
Reference 21), and the UCLA Graduate School of Library
Service used it in its cataloging classes. It is included
here because the Bulletin is difficult to locate.

Tallman, Johanna Eleonore (Allerding)
    Adventures in partial titles; or, You can't find
what you want in the card catalog without this
"catalogers' crutch." Los Angeles, The Author,
1958.
    4 ℓ.

    1. Cataloging. I. Title. II. Title: Partial
titles. III. Title: You can't find. IV. Title:
Catalogers' crutch.

CHAPTER I.   The Parable of the Three Students.

Once upon a time there were three students who remembered vaguely a book called "Public School Finance."
The freshman looked under "Public School Finance" in the
card catalog. He found two books with this title, but the
authors weren't at all familiar. He found two more books
with the titles: "Public School Finance in Minnesota" and
"Public School Finance Programs." These weren't what he
was looking for either. Since he had found several titles
beginning with these words in the catalog he thought that these
were all of the books on that subject in the library.

The senior student also tried "Public School Finance"
and then went one step further; he looked under "School

Finance." Here he found a card which read: "School finance see Education--Finance." He followed this lead and found over fifty books under this subject heading, but not the one he was looking for.

The graduate student was working on a thesis on this subject and he knew that he had used the book before and that the library had it. He tried both "Public School Finance" and "School Finance." He toyed with the idea of trying just "Finance" but decided that this was too broad a subject. He had learned about subject headings and subdivisions, so he tried both "Schools--Finance" and "Public Schools--Finance." However, he was disappointed to find merely more references to "see Education--Finance." He admitted defeat and asked the librarian on duty at the Information Desk. Fortunately she had at one time been a cataloger and knew a trick or two. She listened to the story and then walked up to the catalog and turned to "Education--U.S.--Finance." This was a full five drawers away from plain "Education--Finance" because of the straight alphabetical filing rules used. As this catalog did not have any "see also" cross-references, there was no way to be guided to this entry. After going through about one hundred cards the student suddenly cried: "'That's the one. 'Introduction to Public School Finance,' by Pittenger."

The moral of this story depends on whether you are one of the students or the librarian. If the former, you have learned that you can save time and aggravation by going directly to the librarian in the first place. If you are the librarian, you will hustle to the catalog editor in the Catalog Department and strongly suggest that a partial title be put in the catalog for this and similar titles.

CHAPTER II. Are Subject Headings and Cross-references Adequate Substitutes for Partial Titles?

The opponents to partial titles say that the cataloger should be able to work out a proper subject heading or cross-reference under the words of the partial titles. Let's see what happens.

Again we have a borrower who doesn't remember the title exactly. All he remembers is that it had the word "genius" in it, it was a very short title and was by a famous philosopher, but he just can't remember the name at the moment. So he looks under "genius." This happens to be a word which is also a subject heading for books about

genius. There must be well over one hundred cards under
this subject. He carefully plods through them, but the right
title doesn't pop out at him. He comes to the end and finds
a few title cards beginning with the word "genius, " but his
book does not appear there.

That night he confides his troubles to a friend, who
replies: "You must be thinking of Will Durant's 'Adventures
in Genius.'" Of course, that's it. The next day he takes
the trouble to see how the library cataloger cataloged this
and why he couldn't find it. He finds that no subject heading has been used at all for that book (it wasn't really about
genius) and there was only a title card under the full title.
Too bad the library had not provided a partial title.

His friend, in the meantime, was having his troubles
with the catalog too. He had forgotten the first few words of
the title he wanted, but he knew it ended in "price fixing."
He looked under this and found a cross-reference to two
headings: "Price regulation" and "Price maintenance." When
he looked under "Price regulation" he found at least one
hundred and fifty cards, so he decided to try "Price maintenance" first. This had only about fifty cards. He went
through all of them, but no luck. So he went back to "Price
regulation" and went through all of those cards, but still the
right book wasn't listed.

About a week later he happened to stumble across the
title in a bibliography he was checking. It turned out to be
"Adventures in Price Fixing, " by J. Bachman. He, too,
went to the trouble of checking back with the card catalog
to see where in %*$#& the library had put the book. He
found it was listed under "Prices." "Why don't the librarians
put cards in the catalog under the part of the title that I remember best?" he muttered.

CHAPTER III.   The Case of the New Subject.

When a new subject appears on the horizon a cataloger
has the tendency to put it under an established heading, rather
than working out a new heading. A book entitled "Principles
of Radio Engineering, " published in 1920, was cataloged under
the heading "Telegraph, Wireless." It wasn't until later in
the twenties that "Radio" became an acceptable subject heading. Similarly an early book on electronics, "Fundamentals
of Engineering Electronics, " published in 1937, was listed
under "Electrons." The "Handbook of Industrial Electronic

Circuits, " published in 1941, was put under "Electronics. " The later "Handbook of Electronic Circuits" was put under "Vacuum-tube circuits. " And the recent [1958] "Introduction to Electronic Circuits" was finally put under "Electronic circuits. "

In each of these cases a partial title under the new word or words served adequately until the subject heading became firmly established. We are now going through a similar phase in the field of transistors. At present everything is still under "Transistors. " But books are appearing with such titles as "Principles of Transistor Circuits. " Partial titles are better than a cross-reference from "Transistor circuits see Transistors" since there are so many cards under that heading. It won't be long before we and LC will be adopting the subject heading "Transistor circuits, " but the partial titles are our intermediary aids. We don't feel that they are a "catalogers' crutch" or that we were too lazy to work out the subject headings when the very first book on transistor circuits appeared. We were merely using common sense.

CHAPTER IV. "But You Must Have This in Your Library. It's a Thesis Published at Your Institution!"

Suppose your library cataloged its theses under the author, full title only, and whatever appropriate subject headings the catalogers could assign quickly. (Any thorough subject analysis, with the working out of new subject headings and appropriate cross-references, is considered to be too time-consuming and expensive. "We must keep the cost of cataloging down!")

Now your Interlibrary Loan Office receives a request for one of your theses. The author's name has been erased, smudged, typed over, and is illegible. All you have to go by is a title, which is: "Response of linear systems to non-Gaussian noise. " You can't begin to imagine what the subject is, so you try all of the key words: "Linear systems," "non-Gaussian, " and "noise. " You even decide to try "Gaussian. " But no soap. How are you supposed to know that the full title begins "On the response of..." and the subject heading assigned is "Information theory. "

The same borrowing library, with its poor typist, sent along another request on which the author's name was given as Abrech. The title of this thesis is given as

"Isometric vs. isotonic control transfer functions in compen-
satory tracking of a transient visual target." There is nothing
under Abrech, and, after trying a few of the key words of
the title, you give up. You send the form back, with a request for the verification of the author and title, and even
question whether this really is a thesis done at your institution. You finally get it back with the author shown as Avrech.
You find the author card readily and learn that the full title
begins "A study of..." and the subject is "Automatic control."

How wonderful it would have been if you could have
found these immediately under some of the key words, or
partial titles.

CHAPTER V.   Implications of Partial Titles in Relation to the Divided Catalog.

Partial titles partake of the nature of both titles and
subjects. This makes it difficult to decide on their proper
filing place in the case of a catalog divided according to the
classical division of AUTHORS AND TITLES in one alphabet
and SUBJECTS in another. There is also the well-known
fact that many library users have no clear conception of
title vs. subject entries or even titles vs. subjects. They
tend to think of titles as representing the contents of the
books.

It is for such reasons that it is much more logical to file
all title cards, including partial titles, with the subjects, and
to file all name entries, whether main author, joint author,
sponsoring organization, place, etc., in a NAME catalog.
Such a division makes much more sense and would permit
titles to lend their support to the subject display of the library's holdings.

Except in the field of fiction and literature, titles are
usually not really distinct and remembered exactly. People
may remember the first word, or any of the subsequent
major words, which may be more significant than the first,
or filing, word. If we really want to help the public find
the resources of the library we should not begrudge the
extra partial title cards which are easy to make when the
book is being cataloged. And if your library has or con-
templates a divided catalog, please put the titles and partial
titles with the subjects, not with the authors.

[For an article on filing, see Reference 43, "Manual

Classed Order Filing, Combined with Internally 'Divided'
Catalog. "]

"AND THIS IS SCIENCE TODAY!"

One Sunday in 1962 I received an unexpected call from
Dr. Boelter, dean of the UCLA College of Engineering.
"Could you go this afternoon to Venice [a beach community
near Los Angeles] to the studio of Charles Eames? He has
an idea for a film to be shown at the Seattle Century 21
World's Fair, and I think you can find what he wants. "
(Charles Eames is best remembered for the invention of the
Eames chair, but he created many unusual exhibits shown
throughout the country.)

This sounded intriguing. At the studio I met Mr.
Eames, a serious, knowledgeable person, full of interesting
ideas. What he had in mind was to show the development of
science, and what he wanted from me was a large selection
of interesting covers on current science journals in all fields--
chemistry, medicine, geology, physics, etc. He wanted to
lay them on the floor of his studio in various combinations,
and then photograph them with overhead cameras. The next
day I began rounding up journal issues from various UCLA
libraries. Some journals do not have interesting covers,
just a listing of the contents. But I found quite a few with
attractive pictures and details which should please Mr. Eames.
I brought the magazines to him to look over and in due time
he returned them.

My husband and I went to the World's Fair, which became so well-known for its Space Needle and elevated train
from downtown to the fair grounds. It was time for us to
see the Eames film in the NASA building. There were six
huge screens facing the audience. The film began.

Drawings of ancient, Middle Age through nineteenth-
century scientific discoveries and of pioneer scientists were
shown on the screens simultaneously, with a sound track
explaining the developments. Occasionally the views on all
six screens formed a single whole picture. What a tremendous impact, and technical achievement!

Finally a voice announced: "And this is science today!"
At that moment the six screens were filled with the pictures
of the science journals I had selected--perhaps forty of them.

What a thrill it was to see the literature of science, my specialty, depicted in such a dramatic way. From then on the screens became filled with moving pictures of current scientists, and some of their accomplishments, a kaleidoscope of activity.

This whole presentation was simply grand and I still feel elated at the small role I had in it.

PERIODICAL FUN

Magazines seem to act almost like humans at times. They are born and named (Volume 1, number 1, "Periodical Fun"), they marry (two journals merge into one), they have offspring (a journal may produce a new title as a spin-off from the main title), and eventually they die (cease publication). Some even practice suspended animation for various periods of time.

All such changes must be duly processed into library records. A publication listing many of these changes, called "Births, Deaths, and Magazine Notes," used to appear quarterly in the Bulletin of Bibliography. Recently I read that even this listing has died. Going through the list one day, I was struck by the humor of several of the titles and what happened to them. All of these are real titles, with my comments.

Correct English has been suspended. (We're not surprised, just mournful.) Freedom and Plenty is temporarily suspended ... and it is not certain when it will resume. (We're not certain either.) Zero has been discontinued. (What will the mathematicians and meteorologists do without it?) Authors are lucky for awhile since Writer's Rejects has temporarily been suspended. If you are looking for hobbies and fun you might try Green Thumb, Here's How, Your Dog, or Tour Italy. If none of these entice you, the magazine for you is Why. You realize, of course, that all of this must be pure fantasy since a previous issue of "Birth and Deaths" had already announced that Here and Now has been discontinued.

Here's an example of a publication which was in a state of suspended animation for a long time. It took thirty-seven years for the University of California Publication in Engineering to cover Volume 1, No. 1 through Volume 5,

No. 3. When no more issues were forthcoming after several
years, serials librarians decided it had died, so they closed
the record and bound the three issues of Volume 5. One
day--ten years later!--appeared Volume 5, No. 4, just as
if time had stood still. All records had to be reopened.
Eight years later Numbers 5, 6, and 7 of Volume 5 appeared.
Then it apparently succumbed for good. Seventeen years
later (at the time I originally wrote this story) no further
issues had appeared.

Sometimes a publisher forgets to change the volume
number at the end of the year, and the issue numbers run
beyond the normal 12 for, say Volume 4, and the issues
merrily continue as Numbers 13, 14, 15. Suddenly realizing
that the volume number should have been changed after Number 12 had come out, the publisher labels the next issue
Volume 5, Number 4. Should we librarians go back and
relabel the preceding issues (which had come as Numbers
13, 14, 15 of Volume 4) as Volume 5, Numbers 1, 2, and 3?
Now, if issues 13, 14, 15 were already bound with the other
issues of Volume 4, do we tear them apart and put the three
misnumbered issues with the other issues of newly designated
Volume 5? Is all this getting a bit out of hand? Suppose
we leave everything as it was issued by the confused publisher. But then, how to explain later that there are no
Numbers 1, 2, and 3 for Volume 5?

Some publishers suddenly change volume numbers
drastically. For example, the U.S. Government Research
and Development Reports went from Volume 41 in 1966 to
Volume 67 in 1967. The publisher announced that this was
done so that the volume number would correspond to the
current year. No library has ghosts of Volumes 42 through
66, even though this might appear to be a gap in library
holdings. Now what, do you suppose, will this publisher call
the volume number for the year 2000?

Once I discovered a journal that had several titles
simultaneously, i.e. in the same issue or volume. The
title on the cover was Selected Abstracts from the Abstracts
Journal Metallurgy. The masthead inside started off as The
Abstracts Journal Metallurgy, but then went on to refer to
it as The Abstracts Journal FOR Metallurgy, or The Abstracts
Journal OF Metallurgy. The back cover read The U.S.S.R.
Abstracts Journal of Metallurgy, or The U.S.S.R. Abstracts
of Metallurgy. The magazine came for awhile in two parts:
Part A, The Science of Metals; Part B, Technology of Metals.

My recollection is that the title printed on the spine was the title of the part, but our issues are all bound and I cannot verify that.

No wonder that librarians and bibliographers get grey hair--figuratively speaking, of course!--trying to decide which should be the official catalog entry title. Cross-references had to be made from all of the variations, just in case someone cites or asks for one of the alternate titles.

So many titles are changed by publishers, some of them without apparent rhyme or reason, that one enterprising librarian founded a society and a newsletter to record these annoying items. The society was Librarians United to Fight Costly, Silly, Unnecessary Serial Title Changes (LUTFCSUSTC), and the publication was called Title Varies. This is the phrase used on library catalog cards to record minor variations in titles. The society and its publication finally gave up when there seemed to be no end to these bothersome title changes.

While the society was active it made tongue-in-cheek "Title Change Hall of Fame" awards to some title with many minor changes. The first award was to the Annual of Advertising, Editorial and Television Art and Design, which went through fourteen changes in fifty years. In contrast, Title Varies saluted the Journal des Savants which had only one title change since it began over 300 years ago (1665) as the Journal des Sçavans. The publisher merely went along with the changed spelling of the French word.

For another award nominee I submitted to the society an article called "The Family of Electronics World," detailing the forty titles involved over a period of fifty-two years in a journal which began as Radio Amateur News and evolved into Electronics World. This metamorphosis included marriages, mergers, deaths, superseded titles, variations in subtitles, pseudo-titles and other mutations. This won the Title Change Hall of Fame in 1974 (see Reference 48).

Another Hall of Fame winner was Turkey World, which trotted through such titles as Poultry Meat, Broiler Business, Poultry Processing and Marketing, Egg Reporter, New Egg Reporter, U.S. Egg and Poultry Magazine, Poultry Tribune, Pacific Poultryman, Poultry Craftsman, Pacific Poultry Breeder, Live Stock Tribune, among others.

At the annual American Library Association convention
the society also used to award a prize to the Worst Serial
Title Change of the Year.   For 1973 this award read:

> In recognition of the meaningless title changing
> and meritorious bibliographic obfuscation, Librarians
> United to Fight Costly, Silly, Unnecessary Serial
> Title Changes awards Williams and Wilkins with the
> Worst Serial Title Change of the Year, 1973, for
> the ridiculous change INTERNATIONAL JOURNAL
> OF OBSTETRICS AND GYNECOLOGY to INTER-
> NATIONAL JOURNAL OF GYNECOLOGY AND
> OBSTETRICS.

PIG! PIG!

It was time to go to a meeting in the Research Library.   I felt some trepidation because of the unrest that had
settled over the campus in recent weeks of April 1968.
Many students and also some faculty members and staff had
wanted to redirect the university as a whole into an agency
of protest against the continuation of the war in Vietnam.
There had been sit-ins in the cafeteria, protest meetings,
rallies here and there.   The Governor of California had
closed the campus for three days in an effort to bring about
some measure of calm.   But there was still much agitation
and some conjecture that the city police would be called if
things got out of hand.

As I left my building, I met a friend.   "The police
are on campus!   There's a big melee by the Ad Building.
If I were you, I'd steer clear of that area," she said excitedly.   With some misgiving I headed towards the middle
of the campus.   As I came into the main area I was puzzled
by the absence of students.   Ordinarily the place was jammed
at mid-morning.   An enrollment of 30,000 students usually
meant crowds and long lines.   "I guess they're all at the
Ad Building," I thought and went on with a more relaxed
feeling that I could make it safely to the Research Library.

Just as I approached the library, a wave of many
students dashed across my path, followed by policemen.   The
students scattered in all directions, hiding in shrubbery,
dodging into buildings, or running farther away.   I hesitated
until the crowd thinned out and then proceeded to the steps.

Suddenly a young woman stopped beside me and screamed "Pig! Pig!" A policeman at the head of the steps whirled around and pointed his gun--right at us!

Have you ever looked down the barrel of a gun, with real bullets, pointing at you from eight feet away? In such moments of crisis time seems to freeze. Thoughts skim in split second speed through your mind, yet apparently in slow motion.

Shall I turn back and walk away? Shall I talk to the policeman or the girl? Will he shoot if I move? "After all," my mind argued, "I am a mature woman, a librarian, not a young student. I'm here on library business. I have a right to be here."

Somehow I gave the girl a dirty look--I may even have said "Shut up!"--and I walked up the steps, past the policeman without looking at him. I hoped he would realize that I had nothing to do with the girl, and it certainly wasn't I who had shouted at him. As I reached the door I heard the girl again yelling "Pig."

No one at the meeting seemed to be really aware of the situation outside, and we discussed the subjects on the agenda. But my mind was churning over and over what had happened, how near I had come to grief. An hour later, when the meeting was over, I entered the lobby and noticed some commotion. People standing around were talking excitedly. "What happened?" I asked someone. He said: "A student came in and was chased by a policeman. The student got trapped in the turnstile and the policeman caught him and broke his arm. They took him away to the hospital." The University Librarian, Robert Vosper, had been summoned and he was furious that the police had invaded what he perceived as the sanctuary of the library. Later there were stories of false arrests and general confusion and furor.

By this time I realized that I had actually been close to getting injured or even shot if the policeman had reacted to the taunts of the student and pulled that trigger as he whirled at the shouts of "Pig" on that ominous day.

THE THIRD CLASS BECOMES FIRST CLASS

When I started at UCLA in 1945 there were basically

two categories of employees: academic and nonacademic.
The "academic" classification was reserved for the teaching
faculty (members of the Academic Senate), plus some high
administrative positions.   Everyone else, including librarians,
was "nonacademic." Different personnel offices, procedures
and policies applied to the two kinds of employees.   An example of where librarians fitted in is how they were treated
at one of the social occasions during the year.   The Chancellor gave two major receptions each year at his official
residence.   The academic employees were invited to one,
and the nonacademic, including librarians, to another.

This attitude prevailed for many more years, but
librarians were becoming more impatient about their low
status.   One day in 1966 I had a call from a colleague:

"Are you going to the meeting this afternoon?"

"What meeting?"

"A friend from another department received word
that some people from Berkeley [University Statewide office]
will hold a meeting here to talk about the proposed establishment of a category of non-Senate academic employees."

"How come the librarians were not notified?   We are
the largest group in this category!"

We called as many campus librarians as we could
reach and then rushed off to the meeting.   The small room
was soon filled.   The representatives told us that the university was concerned about the unrest surfacing from a
number of people in this category.   What did we want?

Responding to such a question is difficult when one
has not had the time to organize one's thoughts.   So the
answers I heard were random: "I want a longer vacation
allowance."   "I want a higher salary."   "I want to be treated as a professional."

When word about the meeting reached other librarians
they also became concerned that there had been no advance
notice.   All agreed that the time had come to organize.   If
we had had an organization in place, we would have been
told about such a meeting and could have prepared a position
paper to present to the officials.   But organize what?
a union?   a librarians' association?   a non-Senate academic
employees' association?

In December the UCLA librarians sponsored a meeting to discuss the status of librarians in the University of
California. The time was by now most propitious, since two
university-wide committees--one appointed by the University
President and one by the statewide Academic Senate--were
delving into the rights and privileges of the large number
of academic personnel who were not members of the Academic
Senate and thus not vested with the rights and privileges
accorded to that body. This "third class" consisted of such
academic persons as chemists who did research but did not
teach, doctors who worked in the university hospital but did
not teach in the medical school, people who taught extension
courses, and librarians.

The librarians decided that our profession was sufficiently different from the other non-Senate academic employees that we should have our own organization. We realized
that we needed to develop some consensus of attitudes toward
such matters as job security, better promotion and grievance
procedures, leaves of absence, access to research funds,
opportunity for professional growth, salaries commensurate
with faculty scales, and a voice in university and library
affairs.

It was agreed that such an organization should be
patterned after the Academic Senate. Every professional
librarian at UCLA would be a member automatically. There
would be no dues, since the University would be expected to
pay the expenses, just as they did for the Senate. The members would meet on library time. The association would be
independent of the University Library administration and
report directly to the Chancellor or his designee.

Questionnaires were sent out. Meetings were held.
Committees were set up. When it came time to select candidates for the officers, there was some reluctance among
them to become president. Perhaps there was fear of re-
taliation for this bold move. I was asked to take on this
office, and finally agreed to be nominated, hoping that my
twenty-two years at UCLA and my reputation for straight-
forward, no-nonsense, what's-best-for-all attitude would over-
ride any negative condition. I was elected president for
1967/68, and the UCLA Librarians Association was launched.
By-laws were adopted in September. The objectives of the
Association were listed as follows:

1. To create a forum where matters of concern to

librarians at UCLA may be discussed and appropriate courses of action determined.

2. To facilitate consultation with, and to advise, the
University Librarian on matters concerning ap-
pointments, promotions, standards, rights, privileges, and obligations of the librarians at UCLA.

3. To enable librarians to have a voice in the de-
cision-making processes of the UCLA Library.

4. To encourage the University Librarian to consult
with and to inform, the UCLA Library staff of
impending action and matters concerning their
welfare and interests.

5. To establish and maintain liaison with the librarians of the other campuses of the University of
California.

One of the first items of business was to secure the
official approval from the University to use the UCLA designation. We presented our case to then Chancellor Franklin
Murphy, and he authorized our existence and the use of
"UCLA" in our new association's name.

About this time the university at last and formally
created the third class of employees--"non-Senate Academic."
What did this mean in terms of advantages? Soon after this
was put into effect, it was time for the annual university
budget. In signing the salary authorization, the Governor of
California said, in effect: "Non-academic employees will
get a raise, but academic employees will not." We had
just been elevated to the status of non-Senate academic, and
ZAP--no raise! Apparently the governor had not been told
about this third class. When the Chancellor had his annual
reception, someone in his office forgot about the third class.
Librarians were not invited to either the Faculty (Academic
Senate) or the nonacademic receptions. So much for that
status!

The official approval of the UCLA Librarians Association sparked other UC campuses to gear up for similar groups.
Some had a harder time obtaining formal approval from their
Chancellors, but when UCLA's favorable position was brought
up, they all received approval. Now it was time for greater
achievement.

Since there was already the statewide Academic Senate, why not form a statewide Librarians Association of the University of California (LAUC)? Appropriate new by-laws were proposed and a statewide organizational structure was set up. The approval for the name was received. But, when would the organization be accorded official status as a unit of the university with authorization to advise the President and Vice-President for Academic Affairs, as well as the campus Chancellors? One status we wanted was for the president of LAUC to be an official member of the University Librarians Council, made up of the top university library directors.

I became president of LAUC for 1970/71. Although we established good relations with the Vice President for Academic Affairs, the approvals we sought were hard to come by. Over several years the Association strove to prove its value to all concerned. Finally, in early 1975, the Board of Regents formally approved the Librarians Association of the University of California and all its major issues. In his letter to our then current LAUC president, University President Charles J. Hitch wrote, among other authorizations:

The Association is accorded this official status ... in order to serve a valuable purpose for its members and for the University in providing an organizational structure for utilization of the professional interests and skills of librarians in advising the University administration and in improving intra- and inter-campus communication on matters of concern in relation to libraries and librarians. "

We were in! Librarians were now able to serve on Academic Senate and Presidential committees. They could provide input on library acquisition policies, which sometimes conflict with those of the University Librarians. The president of LAUC could participate officially on the University Librarians Council. The various campus Librarians Associations are a positive force in their academic status. No longer are librarians an unrecognized "third class."

Perhaps my involvement with and pressure from LUUC motivated the University President to appoint me, in the fall of 1972, to head a Committee on Librarians' Salaries. To my knowledge this was the first presidential committee headed by a non-Senate academic employee. Our challenge was to present a proposal about librarians' salaries to be considered by the Board of Regents at their next meeting. When was that to be? In two weeks!

Knowledgeable hard-working librarians, representing
several UC campuses, quickly met at the administrative headquarters on the Berkeley campus. A Personnel Office representative advised us how the university arrived at the librarians' salary scales: "We make a survey of what other large
universities pay, just as we do for the faculty salaries."

Immediately that method struck us as having little
validity for us. Librarians in California do not ordinarily
look to Harvard, Princeton, the University of Michigan, and
others as greener pastures. The salaries of librarians were
generally the same low level in most academic libraries,
so why compare with them? There were better opportunities
nearer at home--larger public libraries, corporate special
libraries, state college libraries, and even some junior college libraries, where salaries were higher. We decided to
obtain up-to-date figures from California institutions. So
we thanked the man and said we would continue on our own.

A member of our committee, Gwendolyn Lloyd, the
librarian of the Industrial Relations Institute on the Berkeley
campus, made a brilliant suggestion. "Large corporations
often compare salaries of their employees within the company.
Why don't we look at salaries of professional classes of employees within the University?" This became a major focus
of our study. And here's what we learned:

1. Out of some twenty or so classifications of non-
    Senate academic employees at UC, requiring at
    least a B.A. degree, librarians ranked near the
    bottom in terms of salaries.

2. Nearly all librarians had Master in Library Sci-
    ence degrees (or equivalent), and over one half of
    them had advanced degrees beyond that--Ph.D.,
    Ed.D., L.L.D.--or secondary master's degrees
    in subject fields. This was a considerably higher
    reservoir of degrees than held by other classes
    with higher pay.

3. Librarians' classifications, as well as salaries,
    were based on the classification of the job, not
    the degrees or expertise of the person. To ad-
    vance, a librarian had to assume more administra-
    tive responsibilities in a hierarchical system. A
    professor, on the other hand, did not need to be-
    come a departmental chairman or a dean to attain

the highest classification and salary, as long as
he seemed very capable.

4. Librarians' salaries rose half as fast as instruc-
    tors on their way to professors. Also librarians'
    salaries levelled off after about twelve years, while
    the professorial salaries levelled off after twenty-
    one years. These figures were based on advance-
    ment as permitted by rules. The result was that
    the life-time earnings of a professor who had risen
    in the ranks was about twice that of a top-notch
    librarian who had also risen to the top. The
    charts we prepared made this graphically clear.

5. The Board of Regents allocated money into a faculty
    member's individual retirement account which he/
    she could withdraw if he/she left the university
    before retirement. But non-Senate academic em-
    ployees could only benefit from the allocated funds
    if they remained long enough to retire.

We also found some Federal government reports which
proved that female-dominated professions, such as the library
profession, routinely received less pay--the well-known sex
discrimination issue.

All of our gathered material was prepared in report
and chart form to prove that librarians should be given salaries comparable to other UC employees with similar education, experience and responsibilities. The bottom line was
that the UC librarians needed an additional million dollars to
bring their salaries and staff benefits in line.

The report reached the president within the two-
week time limit. He presented it first to the Salary Committee of the Board of Regents, then to the full Board, which
approved this increase in the University's budget. So far,
so good!

Now on to the State Legislature and the Governor.
Despite the University's strong efforts to obtain this special
supplementary range adjustment for librarians, the Governor
and Legislature did not approve the request "Extra compen-
sation for librarians--$1,000,000--OUT!" Another ZAP
as far as we were concerned!

The Regents did not forget our needs. The next

year they incorporated the extra money in the overall UC
budget and, at last, librarians received substantial increases
in salary ranges and staff benefits, a "first class" victory.

IS YOUR LIBRARY ACCREDITED?

In 1974 Caltech President Harold Brown recommended
me to become a member of Evaluation Teams for the Ac-
crediting Commission for Senior Colleges and Universities,
Western Association of Schools and Colleges. I have served
on many such teams since then.

There are six such nongovernmental commissions
throughout the United States. Higher institutions of learning
voluntarily submit to accreditation procedures at intervals
to determine if they meet certain standards and can therefore be certified as "accredited" institutions. Those not
so accredited may have difficulty in qualifying for financial
support and grants and in being able to have their students
receive academic credit when transferring to accredited
schools. Schools therefore go to considerable work and expense to become accredited and retain their accreditation.

Before joining the evaluation team for the site visit,
each team member receives a packet about the school. This
includes the college catalog, the report of the previous team,
and the school's self study. The latter is an extensive
document describing the school's purpose, governance and
administration, educational program and research activities,
faculty and staff, library and other learning resources, student services, physical and financial resources, and other
related matters. In addition to reading the section on the
library in all these publications I read as much of the rest
of it as possible in order to gain a clear understanding of
the institution.

The team assembles on the night before the three-day
visit in order to get acquainted and to receive specific assignments from the chairman. He has made prior visits
and provides up-to-date information on areas which seem to
need special attention.

The first thing to realize is that you are a member of
a team. The team works together, shares tasks and information, and tries to cover all aspects of the institution's operation. Each team member is given assignments in accor-

dance with his or her specialty. If the team is small there
may be additional tasks. I have had to look at such things
as computer courses and facilities, audiovisual service, student recreational facilities, alumni achievements, etc.   I
also look for general impressions that can be shared.   Is
the bookstore well-stocked? Does the place look terribly
overcrowded? Is the place well kept and clean?   Is there
provision for handicapped?   Team members can have access
to almost anyone or any document connected with the institution.
Often there is opportunity to talk to members of the board of
trustees.   One can ask for and look at such things as budgets,
salary scales, policies--whatever appears to be an area that
needs clarification.   This provides an in-depth overview that
one seldom has of one's own institution.

A basic task for the team member is to address the
particular standard in the Handbook of Accreditation concerned
with his/her assigned area.   For libraries this is standard
six, "Library, computer, and other learning resources":

> 6A.   "Library holdings, computer and other learn-
> ing resources are sufficient in quantity, depth,
> diversity, and currentness to support all the in-
> stitution's academic offerings at appropriate levels."

By checking through the college catalog I can learn
which are major and minor academic offerings.   By checking
through the card catalog and/or shelf list, and list of journal
subscriptions, I can ascertain the holdings in any particular
field.   In one small institution I discovered that 90 percent
of the general chemistry and 94 percent of the general physics books were published before 1970.   My comment was
that these collections needed current updating and retrospec-
tive weeding.

I encourage other members of the team to check library holdings in their area of specialty.   But I caution them
not to rely on just looking at what books are on the shelves.
The best books may be out in circulation.   Reference collections can, of course, be examined on the shelves for basic
titles.

One component of this standard is to ascertain if
efforts are made to identify and replace lost books or other
holdings.   This can be done through periodic inventories.
We also determine if long-range plans exist for meeting
deficiencies in holdings and if outdated materials are

systematically removed. I ask for inventory and weeding
procedures and schedules. If the library has none, I point
out the benefits that can be derived from such a program.

Another component has to do with equipment. I ask
about and look at photocopying machines, reader-printers,
computer terminals, audiovisual equipment, and whatever
else the library offers to its users. This is a good point
at which to discuss the copyright law and how the library
handles the law's requirements, including copying in lieu of
interlibrary lending and producing multiple copies for "reserve"
use.

I always make a point of talking to some faculty members and students about the resources at the library to meet
their needs. For example, at the University of Hawaii in
Hilo I discovered that the local resources were inadequate
for the level of research done by the faculty. Interlibrary
loans from Honolulu or the mainland took a long time. So
the professors spent their summer vacations at research institutions on the mainland, microfilming resources that they
would need in the months to come.

> 6B. "The selection and evaluation of library and
> learning resource materials are cooperative endeav-
> ors requiring strong involvement by the teaching
> faculty and less formal means of suggestion and
> recommendation by students. "

To me this does not mean that a faculty member has to
approve of every item purchased. In libraries which use
approval plans, it would be sufficient if a faculty member
approves the profile for a particular subject category. Faculty members can and should participate in writing up collection policy statements. (Some libraries have developed
approval "profiles" of subjects for which they desire book
dealers to select the books the library should purchase. This
relieves the library of the specific selection process. In my
opinion and experience, dealer selection often results in a
glut of peripheral publications since the dealer will make
sure that every dollar in his allocation is spent. The Engineering and Mathematical Sciences Library was forced to
participate in such an approval plan for one year. Many of the
titles selected by the dealer were inappropriate. I really
didn't want any book on bricklaying or the history of street-
cars in Great Britain! What I wanted were proceedings of
conferences on technical subjects, but the dealer said, "they're
too difficult to find out about and locate. ")

The library personnel for collection development should be knowledgeable about curriculum needs, budgetary limitations and the collection's strengths and weaknesses, and be able to select most items. The faculty should be encouraged to submit requests for purchases and to keep the library collection officers informed about changes in and additions to the curriculum. When a major program of "weeding" a collection of outdated material is undertaken, faculty members should participate in the decisions.

> 6C. "Books and other forms of learning materials are readily available and used by the institution's academic community, both on and off-campus."

I ask such questions as, What reading, viewing and study spaces are available? What are the hours that library units are open? What are the limitations on hours of access for special services? For example, is the microform reading area available at all hours that the library is open? Do faculty members encourage the use of the library resources by students?

> 6D. "A professional staff with pertinent expertise is available to assist users of library and other learning resources."

A look at the staff list and curriculum vitae of key staff members can give an idea of the qualifications and experience of the staff. I try to talk to several staff members to probe their skills and get their input.

This standard also states, "To assist users, competent personnel are available whenever the facilities are open." This may be difficult to achieve if there are many branch libraries. However, the main library building should have competent personnel (i.e., reference librarians) available during all open hours, including evenings and weekends.

Also mentioned is the availability of opportunities for professional improvement. Are library staff members encouraged to attend library meetings? Does the institution pay for the cost of attending training sessions, short courses and seminars? Is there time available for research? Any point on which the answer is negative and which seems to be a detriment should be mentioned in the team's report.

Standard 6E was added in 1982. It concerns the

quantity and quality of computing services provided by the
institution.

Aside from investigating these basic standards, I
spend time with the director of libraries and staff members,
asking many questions and listening to comments. I try to
find weak spots, or at least areas seen by the director of
libraries or the staff as weak spots. (In some cases the
weak spot may turn out to be the director.) How do they
see the problems of the library? These discussions can
cover budget, space, staff, facilities, equipment, procedures,
faculty and student relations, and other matters that arise.

If possible I also try to talk to some faculty members,
such as the faculty library committee. Team members also
arrange to talk to some students. Sometimes they will
raise an issue that no one else does. For example, at the
Naval Postgraduate School in Monterey, California, several
students said they needed quiet study space in the library at
night. These were students in their late twenties or older.
Although married and living in housing provided by the government, they had small children at home and couldn't do
serious studying there.

Whenever there is a little free time, the team members gather in the conference room designated for their use.
Here are many additional documents. In the case of the library, these may be annual reports, library information
leaflets, special studies, and budgets. There are typewriters
and pads of paper because each team member must turn in
a written report to the team leader before the end of
the visit. For those who can't type, secretaries are available. It is a kind of quiet madhouse as each one struggles
to absorb all the pertinent documents and assemble a meaningful report.

Being on an accreditation evaluation team provides a
marvelous opportunity to visit unusual institutions and observe
them in depth. Did you know that a private corporation can
grant accredited degrees? The first institution I visited was
the Rand Graduate Institute of Policy Studies, part of the
Rand Corporation in Santa Monica. The California Maritime
Academy in Vallejo has a ship called the Golden Bear. On
a tour there I learned that some of the women students use
the machines on board intended for repairing sails to do a
little personal sewing (with the approval of the mate in charge).
The Southern California College of Optometry in Fullerton

has a beautiful new campus, but arranges with the nearby
branch of the California State University to provide athletic
facilities for its students. At the University of Hawaii in
Hilo I discovered a major library problem was worms eating
up library books in the humid library lacking air-conditioning.
At the University of California, San Francisco, where the
medical school was asking for accreditation of its Ph. D. program, I admired its fantastic collection on the history of
medicine.

Other institutions visited were California State College,
San Bernardino; California State College, Sonoma; and Mount
Saint Mary's College, Los Angeles. My next visit, in
October 1984, will be to Northrop University, an outgrowth
of the Northrop Aeronautical Institute, established by the
Northrop Aircraft Corporation. This university is now an
independent school. The library contains what is left of the
Pacific Aeronautical Library where I worked from 1942 to
1944.

I am grateful to have had the opportunity of contribut-
ing to the library profession through membership on these
evaluation teams.

PUBLIC AND OTHER RELATIONS

This story is not about P.R. or how to improve your
public image, but rather about some stark realities this librarian had to face when dealing with a cross-section of
public users and library staff.

Take Student "M." He was quiet, but usually stood
in the doorway of the bookstacks, clutching a shopping bag.
Everyone had to pass him. The staff became afraid of him
because his mind seemed to be far away, so eventually I
asked him to move. "If you're waiting for someone, you
can sit here." No response. I checked him out with university officials and found he was a registered student, and
therefore entitled to use campus libraries.

One afternoon I had a call from the Physics Library
librarian. "We're having a special reception here in half
an hour for Dr. Robert Oppenheimer. There will be refreshments, and Student M is sitting right at the head of the table!
What shall we do?" I called Campus Security and the

Assistant University Librarian for Public Service. Just as
they arrived at the door to the library, Student M moved
away and left.

Another day Student M appeared at the circulation desk
with a pile of books, reports and magazines. The attendant
called me to handle him. I looked at the items and said:
"Do you want to check these out?" No response. I noticed
a current due date in one book and checked the files. The
book was checked out to him.

"Do you want to renew these or return them?"

He finally said: "Renew them."

So we found all the cards, up-dated the due dates, and
then I said: "Here you are; they're all renewed."

"I don't want them," he replied and walked out.

He had been a problem elsewhere, and we heard that
he was finally committed to Camarillo, the State Hospital for
mental patients. We had almost forgotten him when he reappeared and stood right inside the main door to the library.
A friend of his finally showed up and they sat down to study.
When Student M left, I asked the other student what he could
tell me about him. "He's a brilliant mathematician and
comes from a good family. But they've given up on him
because of his withdrawn behavior. He tolerates me because
I can talk mathematics with him."

Campus Security was surprised to learn he was back.
It turned out that he had registered in a summer session
course, which again gave him legitimate campus status. But
too many complaints kept pouring in and Security picked him
up and took him to his apartment, which was filled with library books. Student M was sent back to Camarillo and we
had our books back. It was a sad and disturbing experience.

If that wasn't frightening, here's another story. Professor D had many books overdue and I talked to him several
times about this. Finally, we sent him overdue notices.
Although he said he would return the items, they did not
show up. As a last resort I ascertained the value of the
books and added the standard overdue fine. The amount came
to about $150, for which the Accounting Department billed
him.

When the books did not come back within a reasonable
time I called the Accounting clerk to see if Professor D had
paid the fine. "No, he hasn't, and we have just learned that
he has been let go, so you'll probably get nothing back."

Some months later the Accounting clerk called. "In
checking our delinquent list against new employees, we have
found that Professor D has just been hired by another Department. We can notify his supervisor and him that, if he
doesn't return the books immediately, we will deduct the
$150 from his first paycheck."

That brought a prompt response. Professor D came
into the library, asked for me, then threw the books on the
counter. "Here are your damn books! Call Accounting and
tell them to clear my account!" I thanked him for returning
the items and he stormed out. He had returned everything
except one magazine. I decided to forget about that, and
told the Accounting clerk to clear his name.

About a year after that, I happened to read in the
newspaper that Professor D had been arrested--for murdering
his wife! To my recollection, he was subsequently found
guilty and sent to jail. So add a murderer to my "public
relations."

Unfortunately, there were three persons who worked
under my jurisdiction who committed suicide. One was a
fine clerk who drowned herself in a bathtub over a conflict
with her husband. Another was a student assistant who shot
himself in the head. He was a foreign student and was disturbed about troubles in his homeland. The third was a
quiet older woman, who, over a period of time, became
noticeably disturbed and seemed unable to concentrate on her
tasks. Finally we arranged for a medical leave, hoping
she would get treatment to help her.

After about six months, she called about coming back,
saying that she felt she could handle the work. Although
she presented the required certificate from a doctor, we
agreed with some misgivings. While she had been away we
had rearranged some furniture, added a computer terminal
and hired some new employees. "My, everything is so different," she commented. We gave her simple tasks and tried
to make her feel at ease. But it was evident that she really
couldn't do much. One day her mother called and said:
"My daughter died last night. I found her dead in the deep

freezer." Another tragedy of someone who could not cope
with life.

In another library I was once called from my office
about 4:45 p.m. "L has collapsed!" I dashed out, found
her unconscious, and called Campus Security. The two
officers who came quickly ascertained that she was in a coma,
and they called for an ambulance. While we waited, one of
the officers asked if I would observe him while he checked
her purse to find a telephone number of someone to call in
an emergency. (Presumably they like a witness to the fact
that they take nothing.) The ambulance arrived promptly
and she was transported to the hospital. Later I called
the hospital. She was still in a coma, but finally coming
out of it about 8 p.m.

We learned that her son had recently been killed in
Vietnam and the grief had apparently snapped her mind.
When she returned to work, she could no longer handle even
simple tasks. We arranged for treatment at the Neuropsychi-
atric Institute. A friend of mine was the librarian there,
and she usually had some patients do library work as therapy.
Mrs. L started working there and gradually improved sufficiently to be released and obtain a job with another library.

Dr. T was a friendly professor. He liked libraries
and appreciated what librarians could do for him. Chalk up
a plus for him! He was a physiologist but applied the information to engineering. For example, he tested himself and
others to see how high a temperature humans could endure
and for how long. This had some application to the space
program.

One afternoon Professor B came in and sat down by
my desk. "I have some bad news. We've just found Dr. T
dead next to the building. Apparently he jumped off the
roof." Unbelievable! Why would a seemingly well-adjusted
person who understood the body and stress do such a thing?
We learned that perhaps he had attempted to do too much at
one time: teach, do research, write and publish, speak at
meetings, travel, etc. The pressures had become too much.
That's a valuable lesson I learned from this tragic event.
Don't undertake too much at one time. Learn to say "no"
to constant requests, if the work and time could overwhelm
you.

A temporary clerk, "S," whom we were training

for possible regular employment, seemed to be a friendly
person, quick to learn the tasks assigned to her. We had
high hopes for her future with us and assigned her to help
clerk "H."

One day clerk "H" had to go to the Business Services
building and asked "S" if she would like to come along to
become familiar with that part of the campus. After taking
care of the business, they made a stop at the Cashier, where
"H" cashed her paycheck. Then they returned and "H" put
her purse in her desk.

That night, when stopping to buy groceries, she reached
for her wallet and found that all the money was gone. Had
"S" taken it?

When I heard of this, I asked the Security Office
what to do. "You can't accuse 'S' if you have no specific evidence. Why not transfer her to another department, but
tell those employees to be careful." So "S" was transferred
to the Circulation Department.

This was a more public place, with considerable
number of persons passing through. The inner office was
separated by a glass partition, so everything was visible.
One of the clerks went into the office to get something from
her purse, but the purse was gone! Immediately she called
out: "I can't find my purse! Has anyone seen it?" "S" said
nothing. Finally someone spotted the purse between the desk
and the partition. If "S" moved it there, when and how did
she do it?

The following week "S" did not come to work on Monday but showed up on Tuesday. When I asked her where she
had been, she said: "I was in jail. My sister had me
arrested. She said I had stolen some money from my grand-
mother. But it was my money!"

"How did you get out of jail?" I asked.

"My sister finally dropped the charges."

Hmmmm!

The Security Office suggested that we move "S" again
to another department. Before long, the wallet of one of the
clerks there disappeared. She had carried $30 to use for

Christmas presents for her children.   Since her husband was
on a business trip in another state,   she immediately contacted
the credit card companies about the thefts and telephoned her
husband so he would not use his cards.

There had been no such thefts before "S" came, and
all of them occurred where she was working.   So she became
a real suspect.   Security decided to see if we could catch her
in the act of stealing.   An officer came dressed as a student.
We fixed up a decoy purse with marked money.

The librarian in that area was told to go to her desk
and I would phone her.   She would announce that she had to
go immediately to my office, leaving the purse on the desk
as she dashed out.   The officer was in the nearby book
stacks where he could observe "S" unobtrusively.

Sure enough, as soon as the librarian left, "S" walked
to the desk, picked up the purse, and moved it out of sight.
When the librarian came back she noticed that the purse had
been moved.   "S" said: "You left your purse on the desk,
so I put it in the drawer."   A quick check showed that all
the money was still in the purse.   Had "S" suspected a
set-up?

Paychecks from the Payroll Department were handed
out in one of our offices.   When the clerk who had lost her
wallet with the $30 came to pick up her check it couldn't
be found.   We called the Accounting Office, explained the
problem, and asked them to put a "stop payment" on that
check and to issue another one.

Soon a call came from a nearby market.   Why was
there a stop payment on a check which one of their customers
had cashed?   She had shown a driver's license for identification.

The Security Office told the market to keep watching
for "S" and to check her license carefully.   When she came
into the market again, she was recognized.   When she presented another check, the attendant noticed that the photograph had been cut from another license, and pasted over
the head of the clerk's.   At that point "S" ran out.   (This
is approximately what was reported to me.)

Security called to let me know that the market wanted
to have "S" arrested by the municipal police.   The police

officer was already in the Security Office. Could we arrange
to bring "S" to them without arousing her suspicion? My
secretary volunteered. She gave "S" a logical reason to accompany her to the Personnel Department. There they walked
down the hall, but past Personnel to the Security Office. The
secretary opened the door and said: "Here she is!"

"S" walked into the office and the arms of the law,
out of my life.

WHOSE BOOK IS IT?

"Is this the head of the Engineering Library?"

"Yes."

"This is one of the fraternity houses. A lot of your
books are in our dumpster behind the frat house. A fellow
who lived here this summer just dumped them. If you want
them, you'd better come right away."

A student assistant and I drove to fraternity row and
located the right address. We found the dumpster and started to pull the books out. I looked at each one carefully.
There were not only Engineering Library books but some
from several other campus libraries. Also we found the
same name written in many of the volumes, and in one was a
photograph of a foreign-looking man.

By this time a fellow had come out of the house.
When I showed him the photograph he said: "That's the
guy! He's the one who dumped them." He also verified
that the name written in the books was the same person.

As soon as we returned to the library I started checking the books against our records and found that they were
not checked out; they had been stolen. Campus Security sent
an investigator. After listening to my story he called the
fellow at the fraternity and was given the probable address
of the suspect. As soon as possible I ascertained that the
value of the books was over $1,000, so the theft was a
felony.

In due time the other librarians whose books were
included in this caper and I received subpoenas to appear

for a hearing in the local municipal court. We arrived by the starting time for the day, but our case was not called that morning. When we returned from lunch a bailiff said our case would be heard in the jury room because the court calendar was so full.

We were escorted to a hall which connected the court-rooms and the holding cell for prisoners who were to be tried. Prisoners, some in handcuffs, were paraded past us, giving us curious looks.

When one of the librarians was called into the jury room we could only guess at what was transpiring. At last it was my turn. Inside were the hearing officer (judge?), bailiff, court reporter, prosecutor, the defendant, and a public defender.

I was asked by either the prosecutor or defender: "Can you verify that these books are the property of the University?" He showed me some of the books which had been seized as evidence.

"Yes, here are our property marks, and our book label is still on the spine."

"Has the library lost books to theft before?"

"Yes. When we take our annual inventory we usually discover that some books are unaccounted for."

"What do you do when you discover that?"

"There isn't much we can do specifically since us-ually we have no idea when or how they disappeared."

"Have you ever had a case where you knew who stole them?"

"Yes. Twice I have been called to come to a house where some of our books were discovered. In both cases the person who had taken the books had died recently. This is the first time where the culprit has written his name in our books and even provided his photo!"

No more questions.

Later we learned from Campus Security that the thief

was a former student at UCLA, he was from a foreign country
and his visa had expired. The court and immigration authorities had agreed to deport him to his country.

End of case.

For some strange reason people who take books from
libraries without authorization do not consider this as theft.
Libraries occasionally declare an amnesty day, when any
stolen book can be returned without fines or questions.
Hundreds of items are brought back. But if amnesty days
are too frequent, the thieves will hold on to the books until
the next such day.

Even books that are checked out properly are often
kept long after the due date, and overdue notices are ignored.
The Glendale (California) Public Library recently turned over
to a collection agency a computer list of delinquent borrowers.
A survey of these borrowers showed that 135 persons held
five or more books for more than 28 days past the due date,
representing a total value of $19,426 of books bought with
taxpayers' money. The average overdue fine was $127, with
one patron owing $1,278. Libraries cannot afford to purchase
replacement copies, so the losers are other taxpayers who
might want to read these books. A $10 fee is now added to
each fine to cover the collection cost. Wanda Weldon, the
library consultant who has developed this specialized collection
service for several Southern California libraries, said: "The
common problem in getting library material back is that the
public doesn't take it seriously. The common answer is that
they didn't know it was so important. We get their attention;
that's all we do." And this persistence, and special reminder,
is paying off.

Several years ago I was called by the widow of a professor who had recently died. She said: "Could you come and
look at my husband's books? I believe some of them belong
to your library." When I arrived she showed me into a large
room lined with books. Some were new ones, with receipts
from bookstores still in them. Others had his name written
in them, with no other sign of ownership. But there were
nearly a hundred books which had library property marks
from various institutions where the professor had taught over
many years. And among these were quite a few from our
campus libraries. The widow was aware that these were not
checked out and were not officially discarded books.

We discussed the problem frankly. I offered to write to all the other libraries and, without revealing the professor's name, ask if they wanted their books back. Some replied "yes" and others explained the books were too old or had been replaced. This was a very well-liked professor, but apparently he had considered his need of these books to be greater than the needs of other library users.

In another case a student once asked the librarian for a specific book which he couldn't find on the shelves. She checked and then said, "I'm sorry, but that book was missing at our last inventory. We don't know who took it."

The student mentioned this to his roommate who replied, "Oh, that book. I have it."

"But it wasn't checked out to you or anyone else."

"Well, I didn't think anyone else would be looking for that book. I'm just using it until I finish this report, and then I'll return it."

This attitude seemed to be typical student reasoning. Many of our lost books mysteriously reappeared three or four years after the first missing-in-inventory record. Apparently the students returned them when they were graduating.

Reliance on the Honor Code at this institution does not seem to produce the desired result. I have talked to students who insisted that the Code applies only to cheating or causing harm to a fellow student, but they said this does not apply to the unauthorized removal of books from a library. After all, books are not people, and besides "I need this book." Doesn't that cause harm to a fellow student who might also want that book but can't get it because the library doesn't know who has it?

And remember the professors who had books checked out for many years and refused to return them? That is not an uncommon problem at many schools.

A tip-off led the head of Campus Security to a garageful of books and bound journals. These had been "appropriated" by a former laboratory assistant who had kept his key to the branch library from which he had taken most of the books. When confronted, he insisted that the books were his, but the property marks plus our records proved that

most of them had come from various campus libraries.   Before a legal case could be prepared he disappeared.

A few months later another tip led to a storage ware-
house full of books.   In many books he had placed his property mark and had torn the covers off quite a few others.
(The cover has the library call number label affixed to the
spine and the library's bookplate pasted on the inside.)   It
required a large truck to hold all these books.   However, the
man could not be located.   This time the lock to the library
from which most of these had come was changed.

A few months ago the librarian of this library saw a
man come in and go into one of the alcoves.   He wore dark
glasses and had a beret cover his head.   As he came out of
the area, holding a book, she suddenly thought she recognized
him as the notorious thief.   As she went toward him, he
dashed out the door.   A library assistant gave chase, but
the man had disappeared into thin air.   Where is he stashing
these books now?   Let's hope another tip comes soon.

Libraries have sought to catch people who take library
materials without charging them out by installing detectors
at exits.   These react to magnetic strips or spots placed in-
conspicuously in books.   They can be deactivated by the clerk
when books are presented for proper check-out and reactivated
when the item is returned.

I evaluated these systems for use at the main library
(Millikan Building) at Caltech, paying particular attention to
possible problems and ways of by-passing the detection.
One problem is that heart pacers can set off the alarm.   At
that time the administrative offices of the Institute were located in the building.   They had been relocated there after
the 1971 earthquake had damaged the administration building
beyond repair.   The president and other officials frequently
had distinguished visitors and some of them might have heart
pacers.   What if the alarm rang out and exit gate slammed
shut when that person sought to leave the building?   Another
problem is that elevators might set off the detection system
--and our elevators were within six feet of where the detectors
would be located.

The final reason for my rejection of such a detection
system (other than the rather high cost) was that Caltech
students are noted for their pranks.   (See "Legends of Caltech." Pasadena, Calif., Alumni Association, California
Institute of Technology, 1983.   79p.)

As soon as such a system would be in place, the students would find it to be an irresistible challenge. I am convinced that within a very short time they would have found ways of making the system inoperative by shielding or counteracting the magnetic trigger. All of our expenses and preparations, such as putting a detecting spot or strip in every item, would go down the drain, and the students would have one more victory to add to their list of successful high-tech pranks. Besides, it would be prohibitive to install such systems in all or many of the forty-plus places on campus where there are library books and journals.

I did put in a few guide rails and gates to force persons exiting the Millikan Building to pass by the circulation counter. Here, at least, they must face a clerk and show their briefcases (except for big-shot visitors).

People who steal or keep library books for their personal convenience seem to ignore the fact that these books are the property of the library. Users should learn to comply with the lending system and understand that the library is caretaker of its collections for the availability of all patrons.

IN, UP, DOWN, AND OUT

As an administrator I have had occasion to hire, promote, demote and even fire employees. Along the way I have learned quite a bit about people and how they behave. For example, everyone makes a mistake once in awhile. But it is amazing how few people will admit it, correct it, and say "I'm sorry." If they only knew that this makes them more human and easier to forgive.

Just to confess to one of my own mistakes, I once made some errors in a statistical compilation. Statistics can be tricky and really should be double-checked at least once to make sure they are correct. Somehow I sent incorrect figures to the head of an academic department. After a week or so, he wrote, asking about some of the figures. Soon my wrong calculations surfaced and I had to refigure the data. This time I rechecked everything and sent an apology along with the new report. There were no repercussions.

Some employees apparently do not--or do not want to

--learn from mistakes called to their attention. They repeat
the same ones again and again. Of course, other workers
learn from their mistakes and then become better employees.

Years ago we had a cataloger of Oriental background.
Her supervisor corrected some of her mistakes and was
shocked when the young woman began to cry. I took her
into my office and asked her why she was so upset. As we
talked, it suddenly occurred to me that her ethnic background
made her "lose face" by being corrected. I explained to her
that, if we did not tell her about these mistakes, she would
make similar errors in the future. The purpose of the correction was to make her a better employee. She brightened
at that, but begged me to ask her supervisor to be a little
gentler in her admonitions. She simply wasn't used to the
directness and bluntness of Western ways. I talked to her
supervisor, and the employee turned out to be a first-class
cataloger.

How does one recognize a potentially good, or poor,
employee when considering hiring him or her? It is not
easy. I still think that a good civil service written examination, combined with an oral interview by a competent panel,
is one of the best ways of screening a person's abilities.
I have served on a number of civil service panels and felt
satisfied that we had ranked the candidates in proper order.
Occasionally we have had to question one or more of the
written questions which were poorly worded or the official
answers which were, in fact, wrong. (I once took a civil
service exam where one of the true/false questions was:
"A soft answer turneth away wrath.") There should be
safeguards for a candidate to see his/her corrected paper
and to ask for an impartial review of any contested question.

But most employees in academic institutions are
hired after a review of their résumé and a brief interview.
For a high-up position there may be a panel of interviewers.
In any case, the result is often a subjective decision. What
do you really know about the person's attitudes, relations
with fellow employees, good or poor habits, capacity and
willingness to learn? Would a male employee resent working under a female supervisor?

Nowadays one cannot rely much on letters of recommendation. Personnel Departments insist that a recom-
mender give only dates of employment, positions held, and
salary paid--nothing about performance, good or bad.

Apparently there is fear of legal action in case one negative word is said or implied. The recipient can only wonder: "What are they trying to hide?" And this custom may have an adverse effect on hiring that employee. So you may hire someone who appears to be a good prospect but turns out to be otherwise. Then you face the challenge of developing a good employee, sometimes in spite of herself or himself.

How does one handle a problem employee? From courses on personnel management I learned some effective techniques. One is to listen to the employee tell his/her side of the problem. Then you say: "This is what I think you are trying to tell me," and then repeat her story, per- haps rephrasing some of the sentences. This is called the "mirror" technique. The employee has to face a reflection of his/her words and often this makes it possible to see what may be wrong, and even see alternatives or solutions. The worker will be happier because he/she has "discovered" what the problem and solution is.

If this doesn't work so directly, you may suggest a solution. One of our employees started arriving late every day and her supervisor complained to me. I called her in for a chat.

"I understand you are arriving late each morning. Is there a reason for this?"

"Well, the people I live with are away on vacation. I'm a heavy sleeper and they usually shake me awake, but now that they're gone I just don't wake up early."

"Have you tried an alarm clock?"

"Yes, but that doesn't wake me up."

"Do you have a telephone in your room?"

"Yes."

"And do you wake up if the phone rings several times?"

"Yes."

"Well, then, I'll phone you every morning while your friends are away and wake you up! How would you like that?"

"O.K.   Let's try it."

So I phoned her each morning at 6:45 until she answered.
She did get to work on time, and from then on we had good
rapport.

Occasionally you may have to demote someone.   Perhaps the position has changed, resulting in less responsibility.
(Basically it is the job that is classified, not the person.)
Perhaps a reorganization results in one person, who had become a supervisor, now being put under a former co-equal.
Or perhaps the employee is simply not up to the requirements of the job and does poor work.   Whatever the reason,
it is important that the employee understand what is wrong and
why the action is being taken, and for the supervisor to be
sympathetic and offer whatever solution may be most useful
--a transfer, or new assignment, a course in improving the
skills required, or other possibilities.

Finally, what do you do when you have to fire someone?   The following illustrates how I handled one such difficult situation.   The employee was an older woman who had
worked as a clerk in the library for nearly ten years.   Part
of her job was to file catalog cards into the public catalog.
One day she was seen hiding her packet of cards behind
some books.   She then walked out of the door to the stairs.
Other employees saw her walking out the library door.   She
returned in about half an hour or so, pulled out her packet
and filed the cards.   This occurred several times.   Some
people reported seeing her walking from campus to a shopping area during these times.   In addition to the filing she
also did some typing, but started turning out fewer and fewer
cards, with more mistakes.   Scheduled to leave at 4:30, she
closed her desk at 4:15 and sat, waiting to leave.

I had a talk with her, in the presence of my secretary.   (It is important to have a witness in such cases.)   I
tried the "mirror" technique, but she did not talk about those
absences or her failing work.   So I tried another approach.

"What do you like best about your work?   What would
you prefer doing?"

"Well, I don't like to put call number labels on books."
(That was a task we had assigned to her when her typing became so poor.)   "I really like to type."

"How about filing the cards?"

"No, I don't like that either."

"Why is your typing so poor lately?"

"I have an old typewriter. If I had a more modern one, I would do a better job."

"Well, I recently ordered a new typewriter for another employee. If I give that to you, would you work harder?"

"All right."

She denied going out of the library on walks. "I only did that once."

But she still managed to get out of the office and go on her long walks off campus, she still typed very few cards, and she still closed her desk at 4:15. I had another talk with her, and this time gave her an ultimatum. "You have not given me any good reason for your poor performance or behavior. Your work has not improved even though you have the new typewriter. If you do not make improvements, we will have to let you go."

After consulting with the head of the Personnel Office, it was decided to give her two more weeks to shape up. Then it would be "curtains" for her. However, the personnel officer said: "She is close to her ten-year employment mark, which will entitle her to retirement benefits. There are only two months to go, after these two weeks. If we add up her cumulated vacation and sick leave, the holiday (Labor Day) and then give her an official leave to seek other employment, we can stretch the time to her ten-year anniversary."

There was still no improvement after two weeks. So we had a final meeting. She said to me: "This will be on your conscience and your head!"

"No," I replied. "I have done everything to help you. You have brought this on yourself and it will not weigh on my conscience." After explaining to her that I had no choice but to let her go, I gave her the details of her last two months and said she would receive her paycheck for this time and start on her small retirement pay.

IT'S A DISASTER! OR IS IT?

Earthquake

On February 9, 1971, an earthquake measuring 6.5 on the Richter scale hit Southern California at 6:30 a.m. Soon the radio reported that freeways spanning other roads had collapsed, a hospital had split, a reservoir had cracked and spilled water, houses had shifted off foundations. It was a big one, all right.

As soon as I arrived at the library, I went to the book stacks. The aisles were full of books; some shelves had been torn loose and had fallen over; other shelf ranges had been twisted. The tops of the uprights of shelving showed by scrapings on the ceiling that they had shifted at least one inch.

Immediately we closed the area to the public, started picking up books and putting them on book trucks, pending repair of the shelving. Some weeks later the shelving company came to straighten and brace the shelving at strategic points to prevent future shifting.

Often some good comes out of disaster. In this case the library was repainted, after the walls had been patched up. And, of course, we were happy no one had been injured in the library.

Fire

Early in 1975 I received a call from the manager of the commercial bindery which handled the library's binding. A fire had nearly destroyed everything.

"I presume your insurance covers this loss, as per your statement: 'Insured from the time the shipment leaves your premises until we return it,'" I said.

"Well, no. In this case it doesn't. The Fire Department was slow in responding, and we believe it was arson. Our insurance doesn't cover those circumstances," he replied.

After reporting this to the Institute's insurance manager, I set about ascertaining our loss. Fortunately, our

practice was to maintain detailed lists of every binding shipment.

The list of lost journals was sent to the faculty members, asking for donations of issues to replace these. The
response was most gratifying. It was decided that some of
the material need not be replaced.

By this time the insurance manager reported back to
me. The Institute's backup insurance would pay. I was
asked to prepare complete lists of all items destroyed and
provide the actual or estimated cost of replacement, even if
we did not replace all the items. Also we were to add whatever labor costs were involved.

When all this was done, the total amount of the loss
was estimated at $9,679. The money from the insurance
company was placed in a special account, enabling us to pay
the new bills.

As with any such insurance payments, the insured is
not obligated to replace the exact item destroyed. For example, if a fire burns a sofa in your home, you can use the
insurance money any way you please. Since there were
volumes replaced by donations, and other volumes we did
not want to replace, and labor costs which need not be deducted, the amount of money not spent came to about $4,000.

Well! Let's see, what can we do with this jackpot?
Some of our immediate unfilled needs included computer
terminals, a word processor, and a high speed printer.

"May I go ahead and get these?" I asked the head
of the Accounting Department.

"That's not what casualty money is really intended for,"
he pointed out.

I countered: "But since the money came from an outside source and we have spent everything we intend to spend
for replacements, why can't we use the rest of this money to
buy something we need but which isn't in the budget?"

I won that argument. We bought the equipment, and
this disaster turned out to be quite beneficial to the library.

Flood

Next to the library building is a large reflecting pool.
After a Fourth of July holiday, the first person to go down
to the basement reported water six or seven inches deep.
The water had seeped into the elevator shafts, putting them
out of commission. Soon employees from the Physical Plant
Department brought pumps and gradually siphoned out the
water.

After previous similar floods in the basement (before
I worked there), the library had installed platforms, so
that no paper or supplies stored in the basement would sit
on the floor. But this time the water level was higher,
causing some damage. The water also seeped inside the
walls, and wallpaper was stained and began to peel.

The cause of this flooding was ascertained to be that
someone had forgotten to close a valve of a drainpipe from
the pool. I insisted that the library could not face similar
disasters in the future. Eventually piping was installed to
lead the water from the pool away from the library.

Now, what good could come out of this disaster? I
took a look at the walls in the staff room, rest rooms and
cot room and decided we could use new wallpaper there. The
old paper, of course, was water damaged, and the staff was
tired of looking at the old jungle pattern.

We received permission for this job, since the cost
would be paid from the casualty fund for this disaster. My
secretary and I went to a wallpaper store and picked samples
of appropriate patterns for approval. For the staff room we
selected a pattern of tulips in a field; for the rest rooms we
thought a foil pattern would be a bright change; and for the
cot room we picked a soothing neutral color. To blend with
the new wallpaper, I had the old worn-out sofa and lounge
chairs in the staff room mended and recovered, but the expense for this came out of my equipment budget.

Presto! The basement rooms had a new look, thanks
to this disaster.

Lightning

Could another disaster befall the library? Although

the sky was a little overcast, I decided not to take my umbrella to a meeting in the nearby public library.

A tremendous thunder clap and the sound of heavy rain disrupted the meeting momentarily. But when there was no further thunder, the meeting continued. Afterwards the rain was still pouring. One of the men, who had the foresight to bring an umbrella, walked me across the street to the garage where my car was parked.

When I returned to the Institute, the rain was lessening, and I managed to enter the library building without getting too wet. My secretary informed me excitedly: "Lightning struck the building! It went right by the windows and then hit. We thought a lab had exploded!"

Actually the lightning had knocked off a huge chunk of the grey granite at the very top of the building. Fortunately, the lightning had not hit the dish antenna which links the Jet Propulsion Laboratory with Caltech. The antenna was in the middle of the roof, and wires led from it through all the floors. What would the lightning have done to that?

The granite chunk fell into the reflecting pool and dislodged some of the fancy polished rocks which lined the bottom. Two of the library employees had retrieved the chunk and the loose rocks, brought all into my office and put the chunk on a low table. The piece was about $2\frac{1}{2}$ feet wide by $1\frac{1}{2}$ feet high by 6 inches thick. It had an interesting jagged appearance, an unusual piece of sculpture created by an act of Nature!

Other granite pieces had been scattered over a wide area of the campus. Because of the cloudburst accompanying the thunderstorm, no one had been outside, and no one was hurt. Students and professors picked up pieces as souvenirs, or, perhaps, for experiments. One fellow decided to make bookends from his two pieces.

It wasn't long before word got around that the biggest chunk was in my office, and a parade of visitors came to see it at close range. The Physical Plant Department sent some employees for a specimen. But even their sledge hammer could not chop off a piece of that hard African stone.

Eventually the granite facing on the building was repaired, so that the place where lightning struck could no

longer be seen. But I continued to enjoy this "chip off the old
block" and unusual addition to the decor of my Director's office.

ENGINEERS AND SCIENTISTS

Years of experience in dealing with scientists and engineers and their library needs have led me to several basic
observations. Although it is misleading to generalize, there
are some characteristics which emerged again and again.
For example, scientists are more likely to take an interest
in the literature relating to their specialty than engineers
do. The latter prefer to do laboratory studies or field research, rather than sit in a library and search through the
literature.

One engineering professor had spent a year doing research on a metallurgy problem. While writing his final
report, he came across a reference to a two-volume work
published ten years before in England. The title sounded
important He asked me how quickly I could obtain the
volumes. I telephoned the Engineering Librarian on the
Berkeley campus of the University. She had the set and
sent it by airmail. As soon as it arrived I called the professor, and he picked up the volumes. The next day he
came back crestfallen. "Those volumes include information
I have just spent a year researching. I'll have to water
down my conclusions considerably."

In my course at UCLA on the literature of science,
engineering and technology, this sad story became a prime
example of the basic rule: Make a thorough literature
search before you begin your research.

On the other hand, in 1946 an engineer from the
Douglas Aircraft Company came to me asking where he could
find information on new materials which could withstand extremely high temperatures. Douglas was planning to install
jet engines in its planes and needed to find the most suitable material for the exhaust lining. I showed him how to
use Chemical Abstracts and other likely sources of the information. After two weeks he came again. "I've found
what I needed! We just saved Douglas about $4,000 which
it would have cost to carry out experiments to test the
materials." Now that's the kind of story any librarian likes
to hear!

Scientists do believe in literature searching, but usually prefer to do it themselves rather than rely on librarians. Chemists and biochemists in particular make efforts to keep up and search for pertinent information in the literature.

With modern on-line computer searches, which librarians are learning to do expertly, scientists are more willing to turn to librarians for such a search. In fact, the best search is done when both the librarian and the scientist work together at the terminals. Questions that arise can be resolved immediately, through proper so-called search strategies. But such computer searches cannot be done if the literature needed is in a time period before the indexes for the computer databases start. Also, in only doing computer searches, the scientist is not exposed to the serendipity of having his/her eye spot something relevant in the next item on the printed page.

Both scientists and engineers are happiest with small special libraries, preferably just down the hall from their offices. "What? Go down to the end of that long corridor, or up some floors, or even out of the building to another building?" This is in contrast with humanities and social science professors who prefer large research libraries.

As a consultant to the University of Arizona in 1963 in connection with their new Science Library, one of my tasks was to persuade several departments to merge their tiny collections into the new building and larger collection. I was told: "We are faced with the problems attendant upon calling in several departmental collections that have become rather firmly entrenched.... University policy is actually firming up in favor of bringing all such collections into the new building. This does not mean, of course, that all of our problems will disappear. It will certainly take something more than a presidential edict to prevent such collections from being built up again through the mechanism of personal loans to individual faculty members." How true!

I met with several of the department representatives and pointed out the overall advantages of a single large science branch library. We arrived at a small concession: current journals could be routed to them for a limited time for use in their small reading rooms. I was happy to hear that the merger was eventually achieved.

At Caltech I discovered so many reading rooms and

small libraries that I finally compiled a list which turned out
to have 44 designated reading rooms and library collections.
There were ten engineering libraries. Would they like to
merge and create a comprehensive, fully staffed, combined
library in one location? No way! One professor told me in
no uncertain terms: "Leave us alone! We don't want you
to move our books around. We like our library just the way
it is. We know where everything is, so go away."

When the library administration moved into a nine-
story tower which had been finished in 1969, my predecessor
had quite a time persuading some of the larger libraries to
move in. "We don't want to go to another building! That
would take so much of our valuable time!" Several of the
divisions finally agreed to move in their libraries, on the
following conditions:

1. The collections would continue to retain their departmental names, such as Biology, Chemistry,
etc.

2. There would be no merging of collections. Even
the Physics and Mathematics libraries, although
sharing a floor, did not want to merge their collections or card catalogs.

3. They could retain their own circulation rules and
checkout counters on their floors.

As a consequence, there is no overall library collection
which could be called the Caltech Library. Every card in
the catalog must give the name of the specific collection. I
was able to reverse only the third condition, by installing
one central circulation counter and checkout point on the
main floor.

Science and engineering professors expect to be treated
with considerable respect in accordance with their position.
Who doesn't? When one of them does come into the library
for some reference assistance, knowledgeable librarians use
a certain technique: treat the professor with an attitude that
he/she knows a lot more than you do. Never make the
person look as if he/she doesn't know what to do.

For example, don't say: "Look in the Engineering
Index." This implies that the searcher doesn't know enough
to look there. Instead, ask questions. "Where have you

looked?" If the Engineering Index isn't mentioned, provide
some compliments on where he/she has looked, and then say:
"Shall we try some other indexes? Maybe we can find something more specific." This sounds like a joint search in
which the professor can play a role. Keep asking questions.
"What key words should we look under? Where and how is
this technique or material used? How recent is this invention?
How far back do you want to search?"

Of course, some of them don't want to go even this
far. They just tell you briefly what they want and then go
away, leaving the librarian to figure out just exactly what is
wanted. Fortunately, some professors will be pleased with
your efforts. Others apparently do not know how to say
"thanks."

One example involves a professor who asked for an
article in a Polish journal. We requested this on interlibrary
loan from a large Midwest library which was listed as sub-
scribing to this title. The library refused to loan the item
on the basis that it was the only library in the country which
had it. A request for a photocopy was also turned down. The
article constituted the entire issue and could not, in their
opinion, be copied, in accordance with the "fair use" limitations of the new copyright law.

I wrote to the U.S. Copyright Office and asked: "Is
it really a violation of the copyright law to make a single
copy for research purposes of this foreign article, especially
since the article is over five years old?" At the same time
I wrote to the publisher of the Polish magazine and asked for
permission to have a copy made. There was no response
from the Copyright Office, but in due time we received a
free copy of the entire issue from the Polish publisher.

Immediately I dispatched it through the campus mail
to the professor and attached a note, explaining the many
steps we had gone through to get this for him.

Did he appreciate our efforts? His response was,
"Why don't you librarians get together on this copyright
business? I know the author of this article and could have
sent for it myself!"

"If that's so, why didn't you do that in the first place,"
I wondered to myself. Many professors have postcards or
forms printed on which they can request reprints of articles
by colleagues.

Besides, librarians did not write the copyright law;
they merely must obey it to the extent that its provisions
can be understood and applied.   (For more details, see items
58 and 59 in the bibliography.)

For further discussion on the relation between librarians
and engineers and scientists, see the following references:

1.   Carter, B.   "Problems of libraries working with
     engineers. "   Library Journal 84:1418-1419 (May
     1, 1959).

2.   Hanson, C.W.   "Research on user's needs. "
     Aslib Proceedings 16:64-78 (Feb. 1964).

3.   Sharp, H.S.   "Library and laboratory; partners in
     research. "   IRE Transactions on Engineering
     Writing and Speech 4:58-61 (May 1961).

4.   "Survey of information needs of physicists and
     chemists. "   Journal of Documentation 21:83-112
     (June 1965).

ORDER OUT OF CHAOS

It is no secret to anyone who reads this book that
cataloging has dominated my career from my first professional position to my present volunteer work.   What fas-
cinates me about cataloging?   Obviously I cannot condense a
year's course on cataloging into a few pages, but here are
some of my observations and experiences.

Cataloging is the basic "science" of library science,
established on rules which evolved over many years to bring
order out of the chaos of a mere pile of books.   Cataloging
includes classification by subject, the description of the bibliographic details (author, title, publisher, date, etc.), correct subject headings and cross-references and, finally,
sound rules for filing all catalog cards so that library users
can find what they want.   Now I will discuss only classification as a basic key to the subject analysis and retrieval of
books.

Classifying means the separating of items according
to their likeness and unlikeness; the grouping together of

similar items, the exposition of relations between subjects,
and the naming of the categories or groups. Classifying is
essential in all forms of subject indexing in order to reveal
the pattern of knowledge to the searcher. Such an analysis
results in a systematic arrangement of subjects. When notation symbols are assigned to each category and sub-category,
you have a classification scheme. The classification of books
is based on the classification of knowledge as expressed in
such a classification system.

Philosophers have been intrigued by the universe of
knowledge and visualized it in a number of fascinating ways.
Aristotle saw it as a tree, rooted in logic, with major trunks
representing the purposes of knowledge--theoretical, practical
and productive. These trunks, in turn, branch into the fields
of theology, mathematics, physics, ethics, economics, politics,
rhetoric, art, and poetics. Auguste Comte saw the universe
of scientific knowledge as concentric circles of increasing
complexity and decreasing generality. The innermost center
(i.e., the basic and least complex science) is mathematics.
This is surrounded by a circle representing astronomy, followed by circles representing physics, chemistry and finally
biology, as the most complex category.

Melvil Dewey (1851-1931), a librarian, saw the need
to develop a classification system based on books on all subjects. He divided the universe into ten compartments. Nine
are for major subject classes (100-900), such as philosophy,
social science, language, pure science, literature, history,
etc. The tenth class (000) covers general material for all
subjects, such as encyclopedias. Each of these classes is
subdivided into ten sub-compartments. For example, pure
science is divided into mathematics (510), astronomy (520),
physics (530), etc., somewhat akin to the scheme developed
by Comte. Each of these is further subdivided into ten more
classes. For instance, mathematics has such subclasses as
algebra, geometry, and trigonometry. Each book is assigned
a minimum of three digits, followed, if necessary, by one or
more decimal numbers, depending upon the complexity of the
subject.

Dewey developed his decimal classification system
during the latter quarter of the nineteenth century, before
modern twentieth-century technology and history drastically
expanded the universe of knowledge. He constructed his
classification so tightly that there was little room to expand
except by adding longer and longer decimal numbers. For

example, the entire field of aeronautics must be fitted between 629.13 and 629.14. (When Dewey developed these numbers, the only "aeronautics" was ballooning.) I have seen as
many as twelve figures after the decimal point for some books
published in the twentieth century. So many numbers for one
book is obviously unmanageable in a large technical library.
I favor the Library of Congress Classification System (L.C.).
Most public libraries have stayed with the Dewey system due
to the high cost of conversion. Small libraries like the sim-
plicity of Dewey.

Early in the twentieth century the Library of Congress
catalogers realized that its vast and diversified collections
needed a much more flexible system. They created twenty-
one major classes (instead of Dewey's ten), by using the
letters of the alphabet, except I, O, X, W and Y. The
letters can be used singly (Q is science) or doubly (QA is
mathematics). One class, K for law, has up to three letters.
To the letters are added from one to four digits, and decimal
numbers if really necessary. For example, aeronautics can
have the entire range from TL500 through TL4050, with room
for expansion. Also, L.C. had the foresight to leave gaps
in the system for future developments. Thus, when electronics came along in the middle of the century, the numbers from
TK7800 through TK8350 were available for this subject and
its many ramifications.

The 18th edition of the Dewey Decimal Classification
(1971) is in three volumes, totaling 2,692 pages. The L.C.
Classification (editions vary from volume to volume) is in
36 volumes, totaling 9,807 pages. The breadth of subject
detail and the relatively simple and up-to-date numbers of
the L.C. system make it ideal for scientific and technical
collections. Therefore I gave as high a priority as possible
to the reclassification of books in the Caltech libraries from
the Dewey numbers to the better L.C. numbers. Also, this
conversion process gave us an opportunity to "weed" the collection of obsolete books and use the latest subject headings.

Here seems to be an appropriate place to describe
an earlier reclassification project. In 1950 I took a six-
month leave from UCLA to become the Director of the Recataloging Project for the Naval Ordnance Test Station.
This facility was located primarily in China Lake, about one
hundred and fifteen miles from Los Angeles, but there was
also a large branch in Pasadena where I could do the work.

My assignment was to bring order out of the chaos

of a patchwork of numbers based loosely on the little used
and limited Bureau of Standards classification, which some
earlier librarian at China Lake had decided to use. The
staff and library patrons had found the system cumbersome
and difficult. The chief cataloger had decided to convert the
collection to the L.C. system. In addition to selecting the
best L.C. number for each book, I was to provide the best
subject headings and cross-references, and create new card
catalogs for China Lake and its two branches.

Since the books were in China Lake (except for the
small collection in Pasadena and a very small collection
elsewhere), I based the bibliographic records on the information supplied on a duplicate shelf list record and the sets of
L.C. cards which had already been ordered and received for
most of the books. (A shelf list card gives all of the cataloging information about the book, including the number of
copies and sometimes additional information. The cards are
filed in the order that the books are shelved. This file is
useful in classifying books being cataloged [to make sure that
the book will fit in with the rest of the books in that class]
and when taking inventory. Librarians have a saying: "In case
of fire, grab the shelf list!")

I was familiar with nearly all of the books and could
catalog them without looking at them. I needed to see only
a few less familiar books. These were either sent to me
from China Lake or I looked at duplicate copies in the Engineering Library at UCLA. (I had to work four hours on
Saturdays at UCLA to keep up my continuity of service and
maintain my sick leave and similar benefits.) There was a
half-time typist.

By being free to concentrate on the cataloging and not
having to handle the books physically, I was able to complete
the recataloging and prepare the files in the prescribed time.
The master file for China Lake included cards for material
in the two smaller libraries. Each of the branch libraries
received its own catalog.

Now that my part had been completed, it was up to
China Lake to finish the job by calling in the books and
marking them with the L.C. call numbers. It was during
this process that they discovered some problems. Many of
the books were missing! Research persons had taken them
or mislaid them. And those that were returned were often
different from the information on the catalog cards.

Apparently the original "cataloger" (let's hope it was not a professional librarian!) had not paid much attention to matching the correct L.C. card with the book in hand. There were first edition cards with second edition books. There were cards for a British edition of a book when the book was a later American edition. Sloppy work! The staff had to redo many of the cards I had prepared, or throw out the ones for books which could not be found. But remember, I had based my information on the shelf list cards which were provided for my use and which were supposed to give the correct bibliographical details.

The lesson they learned belatedly was that one should take inventory before redoing the catalog and make sure the original records are correct before relying on them.

The following brief description and accompanying chart may help the uninitiated to grasp some of the steps involved in cataloging and preparation of books for shelving.

Subject Analysis

1. The cataloger analyzes the subject content of the book.

2. Subject terms are selected from an authorized alphabetical list, such as the Library of Congress List of Subject Headings. This list will also help with suggestions for appropriate subject cross references leading to and from the subject term(s) selected.

3. A subject classification scheme (usually L.C. or Dewey) is checked for the appropriate classification and the related classification code (L.C. letter and number, or Dewey number) is noted.

Descriptive Analysis

4. The cataloger now turns to the descriptive aspect of the book: author, title, edition, place, publisher, date, pagination and other details.

5. To convert the author's name to a specific alphanumeric code, one consults a most useful compilation, the Cutter table (see description below).

CATALOGING OF BOOKS IN A LIBRARY SYSTEM

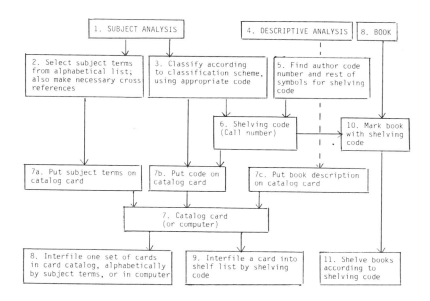

Results:

1. Classified arrangement of books on shelves
2. Alphabetical index by subject terms in card catalog.
3. Classified arrangement of shelf list cards to match arrangement of books on shelves.

6. The subject code (item 3) is combined with the author code (item 5) to determine the basic number for shelving the book, commonly designated as the call number. Since each book in the library should have a unique number, there are such additions as dates (for editions other than the first), supplements, volume number, etc. (If any reader is interested in more details on this somewhat complex matter, write for the author's "Additions to Basic Call Numbers," 1970, 10p.)

Catalog Card

7. All of the information is now put on appropriate catalog cards.

8. One set of the cards, consisting of author, title, subject and related entries, is filed into the card catalog, or keyed into the computer. (The formally constructed subject entries are difficult to program for retrieval from the computer because of length and use of a number of punctuation marks representing special subject aspects. Individual keywords, as coded in the computer, are insufficient to represent the complexity of the subject. A carefully designed and logically arranged subject filing system in a card catalog, with appropriate guide cards, can show subject related works to the user as he flips through the file [see Reference 43].)

9. A card representing the book is filed into the shelf list by call number. (See page 103)

Book

10. The complete call number for the specific book is affixed to the spine of the book.

11. The final step is to shelve the book according to its number.

Steps 7 through 11 are normally performed by library assistants. Now the librarian has brought order out of the book chaos in such a way that a user can locate any desired volume in the library's collection, with a minimum of difficulty.

As for the Cutter alphabetic order tables, they were invented by Charles A. Cutter (1837-1903), a foremost librarian. In the late nineteenth century he created a two-digit code, combined with the initial letters of surnames based on thousands of names. The numbers go from 11 to 99 for each letter. For example, under C one can find the following:

Surname	Table Entry	Author Code
Cain	Cai	C12
Charles	Cha	C38
Churchill	Chu	C47
Cornell	Cor	C81
Cummings	Cum	C91

He later expanded this to a "Three Figure Alphabetic

Order Table, " published in two volumes in 1902. This should
not be confused with an independently developed "Alphabetic
Order Table Altered and Fitted with Three Figures, " created
by Kate Sanborn, and published in 1896. This has evolved
into the "Cutter-Sanborn Three Figure Author Table" now used
by many large libraries.

Once a computer specialist told me he was working on
an alphanumeric code for surnames. When I told him that a
librarian had worked out such a table in the nineteenth century,
he was incredulous. But one look at the Cutter tables and
he was quickly convinced that he need not re-invent this
"wheel. "

Some librarians may say: "That's so old fashioned!
All we do now is search for the title on our catalog computer
terminal and then just go with what we find. " That's fine
with those books which are already in the computer base or
in some other cataloging source. But there are many older
or special publications which are not in one of these sources.
Then you will have to do "original" cataloging--ascertain the
classification number, the author number, the bibliographic
description, the subject headings, and all the other details.

You may obtain employment in a library which does
not have access to a computerized cataloging data base or
other cataloging sources. Also, your library may become
involved with a recataloging project where many older books
will have to be cataloged anew. You may be responsible for
a first-class cataloging job!

If you are intrigued with some of the cataloging problems and their solutions, see these items in the bibliography
dealing with various aspects of cataloging: References 3, 7,
8, 9, 16, 21, 43.

One final word that fits in here has to do with the
value of knowledge of foreign languages, especially when
dealing with cataloging and bibliographic references. When
working in an academic library, one is sooner or later
confronted with a foreign publication. This requires one to
know enough to determine the author and his or her correct
name, decipher foreign bibliographic equivalents appearing in
journal issues, translate foreign references in bibliographies,
so that the final information is correct. (A library, which
shall remain nameless, once listed the author of a German
book as "Auflage, Dritte. " Of course, "Dritte Auflage"

means "Third edition"!) Throughout my career I found
good use for my native German, my high school Spanish, and
my college French major. At UCLA I took an extension
course in Russian which enabled me to deal with titles and
references. For the students in my course in the library
school I prepared a one-page easy lesson in the Russian alphabet.

The tendency of some library schools now to play down
the value of a knowledge of cataloging and foreign languages
is not only deplorable but a disservice to their students, who
should be encouraged rather than discouraged to expand their
personal aptitudes in all directions and thus become a true
professional in a library career.

OH SEE, ELSIE

OCLC is an abbreviation which originally stood for
"Ohio College Library Center, " a cooperative computer cataloging consortium. Libraries are connected with the master
computers in Ohio, via terminals hooked to direct telephone
lines. By 1976 the line had reached Arizona. Pat Barkey,
Director of Libraries at Claremont Colleges, had been one
of the originators of this system in Ohio, and he urged academic libraries in Southern California to join.

After attending a presentation about the system, I
decided that this would be a great benefit for the libraries
at Caltech. Then came some maneuvering within our budget
to find the necessary funds, such as the elimination of two
clerical positions in the Catalog Department through attrition.
Fewer clerks were needed, since OCLC's computer not only
printed the catalog cards but alphabetized them for each of
the twenty-one "receiving" catalogs in Caltech libraries. We
signed up and provided the money to bring the telephone line
some thirty miles from Claremont to Pasadena. The terminals were installed, the staff received the necessary training, and we were entering the modern library world--finally!

By 1979 OCLC also developed an on-line system to
show which of the libraries in a given geographical area hold
a specific item listed in the database. Interlibrary loan requests for the item can be transmitted via the computer
terminal to five selected libraries in the order preferred.
If the first library does not wish to lend, the request goes

automatically to the terminal of the second library, and so
on. This method saves considerable time as compared to
sending requests and responses by mail and compared to
sending requests to libraries without knowing if they own the
book.

A more detailed analysis of this system is contained
in Reference 63. A story in that article involves a request
Caltech received from a small college in New York asking
to borrow the book Surfboard Design and Construction. Our
library did not own this. When we retrieved the bibliographic
record on the terminal, we discovered that the only library
listed as having this book was the U.S. Patent Office. However, the request was sent to five libraries, all of which
were located in Southern California near all those lovely high-
surf beaches, in hopes one of them might have it.

More recently a system for handling on-line ordering
and accounting of book purchases has also been made available. As OCLC became national and even international, the
company looked for a name different from the "Ohio College
Library Center." Because "OCLC" was such a well-known
abbreviation in library circles, it was decided to keep those
initials. The new full name became "On-Line Computer Library Center."

The services provided by OCLC have become so cost-
effective and dramatic, that a few statistics may be of interest.
As of 1984 there are more than 6,000 libraries in the OCLC
system. They are located in all the 50 states and in nine
other countries. The number of bibliographic records has
soared to more than 10 million, spanning four millennia.
The oldest record in this database is that of a terra-cotta
cone with a Babylonian inscription, dated 2150 B.C., cataloged
by Dartmouth University. Besides books, the records include
journals, music scores, maps, government documents and
other publications. All of the libraries are connected with
the computer complex in Ohio through 200,000 miles of dedicated (restricted) telecommunication lines. This a safety
feature since "computer hacks" cannot get into it through
ordinary telephone lines.

In an average week 23,000 records are added, libraries
catalog more than half a million items, loan more than 35,000
items, and order more than 20,000 items from publishers
and vendors.

Young librarians may find it difficult to understand
how things were done "in the good old days" before the computer became an integral part of library processes.

AND THE ANSWER IS ...

A most important and the most fun job in a library is
reference work--finding the answers to questions posed by
library users or arising in the course of one's work.   It's
trivia as well as information pursuit on a grand scale.   The
librarian becomes a detective, looking for clues and following
them, until finally "Eureka. I've found it!" Searching for
answers to difficult questions is an even bigger challenge than
bringing order out of chaos through cataloging.   All one's
accumulated knowledge of reference sources provides a reservoir to tap as needed.   The challenge becomes bigger when
nonstandard or unusual approaches might lead to the answer.

While I was the Director of Libraries at Caltech I
would sometimes ask the head of the Reference Department
if he had some difficult reference question "for dessert"
that I could work on until the lunch hour was over.   This
kept my reference skills honed since I had to use a variety
of old and new tools.   Reference work requires logic, resourcefulness, imagination, memory and persistence.   It's
a lot like working on puzzles.

My training in reference work began in library school
at the University of California in Berkeley.   We studied about
800 basic reference books during the year and had to find the
answers to many carefully selected questions.   Sometimes the
students would encounter each other in the huge University Library bookstacks and ask: "Have you found the answer yet?"
After a particularly frustrating assignment the professor,
Edith Coulter, confessed that she had removed the subject
cards from the University Library card catalog for the books
containing the answers.   This was to force us to find the
correct source in a round-about fashion through bibliographies.
On another occasion she gave us a quotation to identify.   We
went through every book of quotations and sources we could
find.   When the class met again, no one had found the source.
Then Miss Coulter explained.   "This is a question asked of
the Reference Department of the San Francisco Public Library.
No one there could find the answer, and the reference librarians thought maybe one of you students would be lucky

enough to come up with the source. " Of course, through this
assignment we had really learned about many quotation sources.

We were also required to do four weeks of reference
work in the time between semesters. Naturally I went home
to Los Angeles during this Christmas recess. For two weeks
I worked in a nearby branch of the Los Angeles Public Library. The other two weeks were spent in the Municipal
Reference Library located in the Los Angeles City Hall. A
reference question came from one of the city councilmen re-
questing a bibliography on the thirty-hour work week he wanted to propose. This was in 1936 and the Depression was
still a fact of life. Maybe he thought that by reducing the
work week the city could provide jobs for more people.

The librarian asked me to compile this bibliography.
I found a number of articles and prepared abstracts and then
typed the bibliography. But nearly all of the references
were against a thirty-hour week. When I finished the list
the librarian took me to the councilman's office and intro-
duced me as the student intern who had done the work. I
said I was sorry I hadn't been able to find many references
reflecting his point of view. He was gracious and thanked
me for my efforts. The thirty-hour work week did not pass
the City Council.

Reference questions can concern a fact, an identification of a cited publication, a search for information about a
subject, the location of a publication in another library for
purpose of borrowing it, and many other fascinating problems.
Bibliographic citations are often incomplete or inaccurate.
I became so intrigued by these problems that I wrote an
article on this subject (see Reference 17). The actual resources used in finding such answers vary so much and would
require considerable detail to describe that a non-librarian
might be turned off by the recital. Some of the interesting
reference questions I have handled are given throughout this
book, but there is room for a few more to demonstrate how
one goes about the search for an answer or to show the
variety of questions--and questioners.

In the days before flying over the Atlantic Ocean became the way to travel, passengers embarked on beautiful
steamships, enjoying the five-day trip. On one of these ships
was a visiting writer of mathematics from England who was on
his way to UCLA to give some lectures. A faculty member
here had sent him a cable, but back came a wire from the

ship's radio operator: "Have two passengers with same
surname and initials.   What is full name?"

The question was turned over to me since the professor knew only that the man always used just his initials.
It was a fairly common surname.   Now you can follow my
steps in searching for the solution.

Step 1.   Is he listed in any Who's Who or biographical
directory?   No, his name does not appear.

Step 2.   Has he written articles?   A check of indexes
to mathematical periodical articles showed several entries
under the name.

Step 3.   Do these articles actually give any full name
or any biographical sketch?   No, to the first question.   But,
at last a clue!   A biographical sketch accompanied one article.   This said the author had graduated from one of the
colleges at Oxford University, and gave the date.

Step 4.   What does the library have about Oxford grad-
uates?   There is no comprehensive directory, but the library
has a long file of annual catalogs from Oxford.

Step 5.   What is in the Oxford catalog for the year in
question?   Let's see.   Here are the names of the graduating
students.   They all have full names, and HERE HE IS!

Step 6.   Phone the UCLA professor and give him the
good news.

The cable was sent and delivered to the right man
before the trans-Atlantic ship docked.   What elements of
reference work are embodied in this story?   We decided on
appropriate sources to search.   We remembered past experiences, e.g., biographical sketches sometimes accompany
articles.   We followed clues that might yield more answers.
We persisted and did not give up after the first few tries.
Of course, it helps to have a comprehensive library collection available.   How many libraries carry long runs of Oxford University catalogs?

In order to make the best use of what resources are
in one's library I recommend that every reference book in
and being added to the collection be examined by the reference librarian for contents, paying particular attention to

appendixes or special sections which often contain just the
kind of information that may be needed some day. Now put
your "personal computer" to work. By this I mean your
subconscious. It has been shown that neurological impulses
can store and retrieve information if it is put into the brain
as a deliberate conscious effort. For example, in examining
a reference book one day I noticed that in the front it contained a list of the first part of ISBN codes (International
Standard Book Numbers consist of a number identifying the
publisher, followed by a number identifying the particular
book), in numerical order, showing the name of the publisher associated with the number. That information was not
readily available at that time. I realized it was something
worth remembering, so I "tagged" it in my subconscious,
saying in effect: "ISBN publisher numbers are in the British
Books in Print."

The students at Caltech have a traditional event once
a year when the senior students go to great lengths to seal
their dormitory rooms just before "Ditch Day." They barri-
cade the rooms with complicated obstacles or devices that
require ingenuity and/or brawn on the part of the other under-
graduate students to solve for access to the rooms. On
Ditch Day the seniors leave the campus all day, and soon the
other students plunge with fervor into the task of solving the
puzzles. If they are successful, they will find refreshments
inside of the rooms as a kind of bribe not to mess up the
room itself. This strategy is often not so successful. (For
more details, see Legends of Caltech. Alumni Association,
California Institute of Technology, Pasadena, CA., 1983.)

This particular year all of the clues and intermediate
answers were said to be somewhere in the library collections
in the Millikan Building. Soon librarians in all the libraries
were involved in helping the swarms of students follow the
elusive questions. There were many exciting bibliographic
and reference challenges, and the students became aware of
the expertise of librarians.

I found the temptation and excitement irresistible.
The clue I picked involved the identity of an ISBN code.
First I tried the number on the OCLC terminal, but it wasn't
there. Then I tried several likely sources, without success.
As I was thinking about where else to look, my subconscious
suddenly "plopped" the source into my conscious mind: British Books in Print. The basic number revealed the name of
the publisher, an obscure British one. The list of publications

Johanna Tallman consulting a reference book.

of this publisher were not included in the book, nor did we
have a catalog for it. However, the list of publishers showed
an American publisher affiliated with the British one.

With the anxious student following my every move, I
went to our file of publishers' catalogs and found the right
American one. I gave it to the student to look for the specific book with the right number. Soon he exclaimed: "I've
found it! It's Dr. Feynman's book, Lectures on Physics."
Dr. Richard Feynman is a Nobel Prize winner in physics,
a prolific author of many scientific books, and a favorite
Caltech professor.

As other students found answers to clues, the tension
rose. The next step was for them to follow some exotic calculations based on these clues to arrive at the ultimate solution to opening the sealed doors. We learned later that the
students had been successful, due in part to the answers
found by the library staff members, who had also enjoyed
this workout of their reference skills.

Sometimes questions relate to older subjects which are
not cited or listed in current computer databases or in comprehensive bibliographies. They may even involve finding
answers by tapping resources in foreign countries. Here is
an example.

One of the distinguished professors at Caltech, Dr.
F. E. C. Culick, was looking intently through the bibliographic
source books in the Reference Department. Sensing a difficult search, I asked what he was looking for. All he had
was the following citation: "Joëssel--Génie Maritime,
1870." Dr. Culick said he had obtained the reference from
Octave Chanute's book Progress in Flying Machines, published
in 1894. He said the item was supposed to deal with the
measurement of forces on inclined plates. One of Dr.
Culick's special interests is the expert technical knowledge
which the Wright brothers had at the time they developed their
famous flying machine.

After searching in vain for some clue about the author
or subject, I turned to another staff member in the Humanities and Social Sciences Library for help in tracking down the
meaning of "Génie Maritime." (Never be afraid to ask for
help.) She searched for awhile and then tried one of the
French Larousse encyclopedias, and found a paragraph under
the French term. It turned out to be the "École Nationale

Supérieure du Génie Maritime, " an official French maritime
school for civil enginers concerned with naval construction.
It was founded in 1741, suppressed during the French Revolu-
tion and reinstituted in 1794.

    With this information I began to try to identify a li-
brary which might have historical documents on French maritime science.   In a directory of French libraries I finally
found the Bibliothèque Historique de la Marine, located in
Paris.   A letter went out, asking for the identification and
possible location of the item.   A reply came from the Service Archives et Bibliothèques, Service Historique de la
Marine, Ministère de la Défense (Marine).   The reference
was identified as a paper ("Rapport sur des expériences
relative à des gouvernails à plusieurs lames parallèles,
faites dans la rade de Cherbourg sur le remorqueur la
NAVETTE, en octobre 1868") written by an engineer, M.
Joëssel, and published in "La première livraison du Mémorial
du Génie Maritime de 1870. "   A microfilm copy was ordered
and received.   The report contained early data on the forces
exerted on surfaces in steady flow.   M. Joëssel was interested in the force and its effective location on ship rudders
deflected at various angles.   Dr. Culick was delighted; it
was exactly the information he had been searching for.   If
he published a reference to this item, I asked him, as a
favor, to please give the complete identification, so that
future librarians wouldn't have to go through my long search.

    Consultation can be considered as sophisticated ref-
erence work since the company, organization or person
hiring you wants solid answers to tough problems.   My consultation work has included such assignments as these:

●   Survey of all aspects of specific corporate libraries.

●   Appraisals of current market value of large quantities
    of journals donated to libraries, with due regard to
    I.R.S. regulations.

●   Analysis over a period of time of current scientific
    and engineering articles to identify recent develop-
    ments in materials, processes, equipment and
    services.

●   Preparation of information on indexing and abstracting
    services for serial publications. This was part of
    a document to train library personnel in reference
    work.   (See Reference 38.)

• Determination of the value of a complete technical
  library which was to be sold to an interested party.

Many of the consulting jobs concerned library space
problems--layout, equipment, and difficulties due to architectural matters. A company was relocating into the 39th
floor of an office building and I was asked to give advice on
the layout of the library in the space assigned. The main
problem was the location of six huge rotary electric files.
Each was 8 feet 3 inches wide, 9 feet high, and 41 inches
deep. These contained files which were consulted frequently.
When full, the weight of each file was 6,500 pounds! Their
sheer size might overpower the rest of the small library.

From the building's engineers I received assurance
that the floors could bear this amount of concentrated dead
weight. From the building floorplan I learned that there was
one large column in the room and a half column on one side,
so I would have to take these into consideration. I placed
the files at the rear of the space, then placed seven-shelf-
high bookcases in front of them, with plants on top, to hide
them further. An opening for access was placed in the middle.

Reading and index tables, normal files, counter-height
shelving and the card catalog filled the rest of the library
work area. The circulation counter was placed at the en-
trance/exit and office areas along the front wall, with a semi-
private glassed-in office for the head librarian. The library
was laid out nearly as planned. I have visited it several
times, feeling "at home" as soon as I enter. The big files
are so well camouflaged that one is not aware of them.

A more involved consulting request was to provide a
complete survey of the technical library of a research and
manufacturing company. I arranged for a series of weekly
visits (using my vacation allowance), each followed by a detailed written report, with a final discussion at the end with
the Library Committee.

The purpose of this survey was to provide the Library
Committee with the following information:

1. A detailed, impartial and professional analysis
    of the existing library, its organization   size,
    collection, staff, services, procedures, etc.

2. Comparisons with similar libraries and with li-
    brary standards.

3. Recommendations for immediate consideration, to
    bring about the best possible operation and serv-
    ice in the immediate future.

4. Suggestions of a more general nature for desirable
    or possible changes, expansion, services, policies,
    layout, equipment, etc., in the more distant future.

At the first meeting I asked the Committee where the
library stood in relation to the rest of the company, specifically where it fitted in the organization chart.   "We have
no organization chart," I was informed.   So I asked about the
supervisor to whom the librarian reported and to whom he
reported, and on up to the top.

It turned out that, although the library served many
sections and departments including the corporate office, it
was at the bottom, along with the Model Shop, Drafting, Technical Writing, and Engineering Records.   The Technical Library reported to Engineering Services, which reported to
Research and Engineering, which reported to the manager of
the Scientific Instruments Division, which reported to the top
executives.   This placement of a corporate library is not
unusual, but that doesn't make it right.

My recommendation was to put the library directly
under the manager of the Scientific Instruments Division, so
that the library's budget, needs, location and other matters
could be planned in relation to its total services to all areas
of the company.

My subsequent review and recommendations covered
such matters as the layout of the library space for most
effective use; the quality and nature of the collections; budget;
equipment; the library staff and its services; library procedures and records; and the library from the point of view
of the users.   The Library Committee seemed to understand
what I was pointing out and recommending.   Many of my
suggestions were subsequently implemented.

It is obvious that no one can know everything in the
world.   But a good reference librarian knows where to look
and how to go about finding the answers.

MORE, MORE--FASTER, FASTER--HELP, HELP!

In 1958 famed science-fiction writer Isaac Asimov

published a nonfiction book entitled Only a Trillion (New York: Schuman). In this he described a number of scientific facts which are recorded in extremely large numbers. For example, how long do different atoms exist? How many carbon atoms are in a person's genes? How many red blood corpuscles are in one drop of blood? How much luck was involved in the development, on earth, of life from nonliving substances?

One chapter, "The Sound of Panting," dealt with the extent of the scientific literature that he, as a biochemist, needed to read to keep up with new developments. There were textbooks, monographs, journals, reports, review articles, annual reviews, conference proceedings, abstracts-- each demanding attention. He estimated that the number of papers of biochemical interest appearing in journals amounted to 2,500 each month! He ended by saying: "If you are ever up Boston way, and hear the sound of panting, you may think it is the result of my chasing some female around some desk--but you'd be wrong. It's just Asimov trying to keep up with the literature, a task which is much more futile and far less likely to reach a satisfactory conclusion (Only a Trillion, pp. 145-155).

Scientists have been sharing scientific discoveries through journals since January 5, 1665, when a Frenchman, Denis de Sallo, began publishing a weekly journal which included letters, reviews of books, and abstracts of decrees. He called it the Journal des Sçavans (see Martha Ornstein's The Role of Scientific Societies in the 17th Century. 3rd ed. University of Chicago Press, 1938, pp. 198-209). The word "journal" comes from the French word for "day"--"jour"-- and was intended to be a kind of diary of new scientific developments. Such a publication permitted a scientist to keep up with intellectual developments throughout the world.

Evidently the time was ripe for a journal made up of brief communications since just two months later the Royal Society began publishing its Philosophical Transactions. The word "Philosophy" at that time referred to natural science, encompassing the fields of mathematics, astronomy, physics, chemistry, natural history, physiology and biology. Chemists were among the first scientists to establish journals in their specialty, beginning in 1778 with Chemisches Journal. From then on the scientific literature, with longer articles, mushroomed at prolific rates. Before long, abstract journals became popular since it was increasingly difficult for the scientists to keep up with all the new publications.

Nearly always scientists cite previous relevant works
to show what has been done up to that time.   Even Albert
Einstein in his famous paper, "Die Grundlagen der Allgemeinen
Relativitätstheorie" (The principles of the general relativity
theory), refers to no fewer than seventeen previous writers
whose work contained something he found useful in developing
his theory.   (See Annalen der Physik, 49:769-822 [1916]).

Sir Isaac Newton used a quotation, already famous in
his day, to acknowledge the contributions of his contemporar-
ies in a letter to fellow scientist Robert Hooke: "What Des-
Cartes did was a good step.   You have added much in several
ways, and especially in taking the colours of thin plates into
philosophical consideration.   If I have seen further it is by
standing on the shoulders of giants" cited in Dictionary of
Scientific Biography, 1974, vol. 10, p. 55).   Another expression of this concept of the continuity of scientific thought is
by C. De Santillana: "We conclude that what looked to us
like a point of departure is only a phase in a line of thought
which stretches back into the dim regions of predynastic
origins everywhere" (The Origins of Scientific Thought, from
Anaximander to Proclus, 600 B.C. to 300 A.D. University
of Chicago Press, 1961, p. 12).

This cumulative accretion of scientific information is
described by historian of science Derek de Solla Price as a
pile of bricks.   "Each researcher adds his bricks to the pile
in an orderly sequence that is, in theory at least, to remain
in perpetuity as an intellectual edifice built by skill and arti-
fice, resting on primitive foundations, and stretching to the
upper limits of the growing research front of knowledge."

He also determined that the size of the labor force of
science has increased exponentially along with the literature,
so that "80 to 90 percent of all scientists that have ever
been, are alive now." If such growth continues, he foresees
that the problem with the literature and the science manpower
will become acute, a symptom of a deep-rooted disease of
science.   He suggests some solutions in the chapter "Diseases
of Science, " in his book Science Since Babylon (New Haven:
Yale University Press, 1961, pp. 92-124).

An example of the vastness of such bibliographic links
is the Science Citation Index.   The 1983 index lists 566,671
source items, based on writings of 1,561,971 authors.
These source items cite previous relevant articles, books,
patents, etc., totaling 8,737,642 citations.

In the year 1980 <u>Chemical Abstracts</u> cited 548,676 papers, patents, and other documents. Over 14,000 scientific and technical periodicals with possibilities of chemical contents are monitored by <u>Chemical Abstracts.</u> There are about 25,000 currently published scientific and technical periodical titles which can be considered scientific research journals. In Dr. Asimov's field of biochemistry there are about 115 journals, resulting in more than 100,000 abstracts a year. If he were to read one abstract every five minutes, every hour of every day, for one year, he could just about read all of these. But he would have no time to sleep, eat, write, or do all those things which make life worthwhile. So what does a scientist do these days to keep up with the literature in his/her specialty?

One can, for example, rely on computerized bibliographic database searching. All of the abstracts are now put into on-line bases and can be searched by keywords combined with such specified limitations as language, dates, specified journals, authors, etc. The searches can be narrowed through certain logical combinations. The result is that the most specific references and abstracts are retrieved. Samples can be viewed on a screen or printed, and if they seem to be on target, the rest can be printed off-line at a reduced price. Often the article itself can be ordered on-line on the computer terminal from the agency supplying the database.

Another way of zeroing in on the best current relevant articles is to start with an older article on the subject and then use a kind of reverse bibliography which lists subsequent articles that have referred to the original article. These bibliographic links provide a tremendous network of related information. They are captured in the immense publication called <u>Science Citation Index.</u> (See above-mentioned statistics.) In addition to these links, the source articles are indexed by the use of keywords called "permuterms" for a comprehensive subject approach.

Now a scientist like Dr. Asimov can find the latest information on his specialty, not by running to keep up with the journals and abstracts at random, but by walking to his nearest science library to have a computer search made or to use the various comprehensive special indexes. Real help is at hand!

GUIDELINES FOR PROFESSIONAL DEVELOPMENT

From time to time young librarians ask me for advice
on how to get ahead. Here are some of the principles which
have worked for me. They are not necessarily in priority
order.

1. Enjoy your work. If you're going to work from
8 to 5 for forty years or more, you'd better like what you're
doing. If you don't, you might as well look for some other
more compatible work.

2. Learn by observation. When you visit other es-
tablishments in your line, look for anything useful--layout,
equipment, forms, signs, procedures, files, etc. Make
notes of impractical items to avoid, as well as suitable ones
to consider.

3. Keep up with new developments. When I started,
there were no modern copying machines (just ditto or hecto-
graph). There were no computers for library operations,
no microfiches, no punched cards, no phone modems, no
electric typewriters (not to even dream of electronic typewriters or printers), no personal computers, no word proc-
essors, no cathode ray tubes, no on-line systems. As all
of these things came along, librarians had to attend work-
shops, seminars, conferences, exhibits, courses, training
programs, etc., to learn by "hands-on" experience, in order
to arrive at decisions which would work best for their particular operations.

4. Plan ahead. One thing leads to another. What
will the effects be down the line from your decisions today?
Consider all possible angles. It's a little like playing chess.
Besides making sure of details, try to see the larger frame-
work.

5. Be fair and considerate. As an employee, department head, or the Big Boss, you will frequently need to
relate to and evaluate other employees or your superiors.
If you can't agree on something, at least try to see their
point of view. Don't be dictatorial but firm when necessary.
As a boss, be available to your staff and listen to what they
have to say. You might learn something worthwhile.

6. Learn how to write effective reports and use
statistics properly. Reports are used to record the status of

the library and its operations; to explain the library's achievements as well as problems; to create a clear image that readers of the report will grasp. Correct statistics, displayed in
a meaningful way, can greatly enhance the written text. Be
accurate and honest. Just because your library did not reach
the goal of another million volumes does not mean you can
manipulate the figures to your advantage. Sheer size isn't
everything. Besides, the facts will eventually catch up with
you.

7. Become active in organizations. Each profession
has organizations where you can meet other professionals.
By becoming active, as a cimmittee member, chairman,
or officer, your knowledge and horizons will be greatly expanded. And think of what that participation will do to your
résumé! Learn how meetings are conducted, how to use
parliamentary procedures correctly, how by-laws work. Then,
some day, you may discover that you're the leader.

8. Follow--and create--opportunities. If you are
offered an opportunity to take a leave of absence to do another job for awhile, to travel, to attend a distant conference,
to teach, to accept a challenging job, to be a consultant, to
serve in a special capacity--do it! It will enrich your career.

PART III:

BRAZIL VIGNUTS, WITH A TWIST OF LIME

THE FULBRIGHT CONNECTION

In February 1966 I received a letter from the Committee on International Exchange of Persons in Washington, D.C., asking if I would be interested in applying for a Fulbright lectureship at the University of São Paulo, Brazil. My name had been suggested by Dr. J. Richard Blanchard, then Librarian of the University of California, Davis. The lectures would be on scientific documentation, and the courses could be given in English. The lectures were based on the graduate course I had taught at UCLA for a number of years on the literature of science, engineering and technology. The Committee assists the U.S. Department of State in administrating the academic exchanges for university lecturing and advanced research.

After consideration of professional and personal matters, I filed the necessary application and related papers. Soon confirmation came that the Committee had acted favorably on this application as a candidate. In July a letter came from Rio de Janeiro from the Brazilian arm of the Fulbright Commission, informing me that I had been selected for a grant by the Board of Foreign Scholarship under the Fulbright-Hays Act. The basic purpose of this program is to increase the mutual understanding between people of the United States and Brazil through exchange of students, teachers, lecturers and research scholars. I signed the grant authorization and final preparations got under way. I agreed to a period of six months.

The Commission requires that one's home institution

arrange a sabbatic leave or similar arrangement to provide additional funds, since the Fulbright stipend is often less than one's regular salary. Librarians at UCLA were not entitled to such sabbatic leave, but University Librarian Robert Vosper arranged for me to receive two months leave with pay to assist me with such continuing expenses as taxes, insurance and mortgage payments.

The assignment had been changed to spend three months in Rio de Janeiro as a lecturer in the Instituto Brasileiro de Bibliografia e Documentação (I.B.B.D.), and then go to São Paulo for the final months to assist in setting up a library for the new School of Cultural Communications at the University of São Paulo. My husband, Lloyd, was retired and could go along (at his expense) to keep me company and see what Brazil was really like.

The State Department required that we spend a day or two in Washington while en route to Brazil for a brief predeparture orientation session. The State Department also authorized Pan American to issue me a prepaid ticket from Los Angeles to Washington to New York and thence to Rio.

The orientation in Washington was brief, informal but helpful in a general way. One problem was that the State Department had told us that our Brazilian visas could be obtained in Washington because it would be easier. However, they sent us to the Brazilian Embassy Visa Office at a time when it was closed for the day (3 p.m.), and we were informed by an attendant that it normally takes 48 hours to process a visa application. We pleaded and showed our flight tickets, indicating our departure in less than 48 hours. The attendant said to leave our request and return the next day when the Visa Office was open. We called ahead and were told that if we came later in the day the visas would be ready-- and they were.

After we had been in Brazil for awhile we realized that the orientation could have been more extensive. For example, we could have used city maps, information on public transportation, lists of restaurants of various kinds, etc. Also, as a visiting professional, I would have liked to have received introductions to professional colleagues in the host country, perhaps at a social function such as a lunch, invitations to attend professional activities, and escorted trips to interesting spots in the city and environs. These are the kinds of activities Americans customarily extend to visiting

foreign scholars, to be helpful in assisting the newcomer to
become acquainted with his/her new "home. " A passing ob-
lique reference by one of the "orienters" in Washington, that
"Brazilians think Americans are over-organized, " hardly led
us to anticipate that no such courtesies would be extended to
us. Orienting oneself in a metropolitan city in a foreign
country, whose language one does not speak, can be both
frustrating and frightening. Some kind of planned orientation at the local level would have created better understanding
of and insight into local customs, procedures and attitudes.

My experience at the I. B. B. D. proved to be difficult.
The person designated as my translator and coordinator was
busy with other assignments and could devote little time to
me or my program. Midway in the program she quit translat-
ing for me and we used one of the students, who very kindly
took over the task.

When I arrived at the I. B. B. D. I was informed that
my lectures on the scientific literature were not needed.
What they wanted was anything on library mechanization--the
word used before "automation" bacame popular. I wrote immediately to colleagues in the U. S. to send me specialized,
current reports and examples on library mechanization projects. A series of lectures was agreed upon, incorporating
some of my original syllabus material, plus a number of new
lectures. Very little source material was available in the
I. B. B. D. library, so I sent to the U. S. for some books and
publications which I gave to the Institute when I left.

Although the librarians at the I. B. B. D. told me they
were interested in library mechanization, they did not attend
my lectures on these subjects. Only the graduate students
who were enrolled took the courses. Several times I tried
to organize a discussion group or seminar for the I. B. B. D.
staff, but arrangements were never concluded. I talked to
individual section heads to find out what their mechanization
plans and problems were. I could not elicit specific comments
indicating any concrete thinking and planning. The mere acquisition of a "Flexowriter" or micro-image reader does not
add up to "mechanization. "

Another difficulty was lack of work space. I had a
desk piled high with someone else's books and papers. During one week, while a seminar on scientific documentation was
in progress, my desk was not available at all. I was neither
invited to sit in on the seminar nor even told about it in

advance. My lecture notes were supposed to be copied, typed
and reproduced for the students. With the exception of a few
lectures, this was not done. There was always some reli-
gious or national holiday, so often there were no classes. I
spent time visiting other libraries.

Early in November I told the Fulbright Commission that
my lectures would be concluded by the end of the month and
that I was anxious to begin my assignment in São Paulo on
December first. This was agreeable to them. When I arrived there I was told that December was an inconvenient
month because everyone was on summer vacation. There
was no mention of the Institute of Cultural Communications
or setting up a library for it. Instead I was asked to give
my "Rio" lectures to a group of Paulista librarians, mostly
from the university-related libraries. It was not until January, after repeated inquiries, that I was told that the Institute director had just been appointed, that he did not even
have office space and had no plans to have a library started
at this time. There was apparently lack of communication
and follow-up on the original idea to have me set up a library for an institute which was in the early formulation
stages.

At this point Dr. Gaston Litton, the other Fulbright
grantee in library science at the University of São Paulo,
invited me to give some of my lectures to his large class.
This class was just reaching the subject of library mechanization, so my lectures fit in. He acted as interpreter.

After that I visited a number of libraries not only in
São Paulo but also in such cities as Belo Horizonte and Pôrto
Alegre, and did some other traveling, all with the approval
of the Fulbright Commission.

The projected trip to the capital city, Brasília, did
not take place either. In December I had been asked to go
there for the last week of our stay to talk to the students
in the university's library school. In February, when I
asked about travel and accommodation arrangements, I was
told: "There is no place to stay because that is the time
the new president of Brazil is to be inaugurated and all hotels
will be full." Surely they knew this in December. When I
asked if some faculty member couldn't accommodate us, we
were told that Brazilians don't do that. We flew home to
the U.S. from São Paulo on March 15, 1967.

My trip to Brazil enabled me to see a foreign country

and its culture over an extended period of time. This experience expanded my understanding and fulfilled one of the
aims of a Fulbright grant. I also had many occasions to
talk with librarians, see their facilities and share my professional knowledge with them. For these opportunities I
am most grateful to the Fulbright Educational Exchange Program.

The following vignettes (or Brazilian "vignuts") illustrate some of the culture shock we experienced and our re-
actions to living in this country where we did not speak the
native language, Portuguese. In spite of the "twist of lime,"
these stories are not meant to be a put-down of Brazil. We
met some wonderful people and saw unusual sights. Rather
than the usual travelog, this is an account of our particular
experiences.

FLYING DOWN TO RIO

It was after midnight when the plane finally took off
from Kennedy Airport in New York. There had been a delay
of several hours due to some mechanical problem. We were
too excited to sleep much; besides, there was little room to
stretch out. By the time dawn arrived and the sun was a
red glow in the eastern sky, we were already over the ocean
nearing Brazil, flying down to Rio.

As the plane banked slowly and started to descend, we
saw many dark mountain peaks, between which were innumer-
able buildings tightly packed in the limited space. Soon appeared a long broad beach with tall buildings edging it. Could
that be Copacabana? And there, on the tallest peak, was
the statue of Christ the Redeemer, with arms spread ninety
feet. Quickly we landed and arrived at Galeõ, the international airport.

But to us this looked more like some small sleepy-
town airport of forty years ago: no big airport terminal
building, no taxi stands, no hustle and bustle, just a dreary
line-up for customs inspection. As we came through the door
into the small lobby, we were greeted by our host, a Brazilian from the local office of the Fulbright Commission. He
took us to a waiting car, and we were off into our Brazilian
adventure.

He drove a long way past industrial districts, ships

in ports, and then through downtown with tall modern business
buildings. We continued along a green parkway next to the
bay, through some tunnels, and suddenly there was Copacabana
Beach. Our hotel turned out to be the "California." Here we
had just left California. Couldn't Fulbright officials have
picked a hotel with a more Brazilian name? The hotel beds
were so short that we had to curl up to get our toes in.
There were no bed springs--only a hard mattress on wooden
slats. Lloyd called the pillows "soft rocks."

As we began to experience life in Brazil, I started a
diary of my impressions. So here are my vignettes--Brazil
nuts or "vignuts"--with now and then a little twist of bitter
lime.

COPACABANA BEACH

The words "Copacabana Beach" waft images of a crescent
golden strand, white surf, happy sunbathers, blue sky, Sugar
Loaf Mountain in view, wide sidewalks with undulating black
and white patterns, and an endless row of high-rise hotels
and apartments, where wealthy Brazilians and tourists can
drink in all this, with perhaps a cup of Brazilian cafézinho
on the side. And that is what we found--almost!

The view is there, on sunny days. The sunbathers
include a motley group of beachniks, yé-yé youngsters, old-
sters taking walks, and dogs doing likewise--and more. Few
people are in the surf; some surfriders have a corner at the
extreme end of the beach. The sidewalks deserve a "vignut"
all to themselves. There are some grand hotels like the
Copacabana Palace and some that are nothing special. But
there are also automobile salesrooms, schools, many crumb-
ling walls and old deteriorating houses, outdoor cafés, and
many run-down apartments and smaller hotels. The traffic
on the street between the beach and the edifices is part of
the fantastic, wild, unbelievable Rio pattern.

But what is behind this frontage? On side and parallel streets, squeezed in before one of Rio's many monolithic
mountains, are banks, shops, restaurants, magazine vendors,
arcades, vegetable and fruit stands, business buildings, swirls
of people, cars parked helter-skelter, street cars and buses.
Small crews work at polishing brass, picking flaked paint,
or brushing liquid to cover up deterioration, making sure to

splatter some on the obvious tourist couple who are purposely giving the ladder a wide berth.

The heat, noise, strange odors, zipping cars, broken sidewalks, all assail our unconditioned senses. There is so little of charm or attractiveness, nothing to invite relaxation.

After five days, with experiences on a rush-hour bus, cab rides in ancient Chevys, Volkswagens and "57" varieties of second-hand dealers' rejects, we bid farewell to this fabulous tourist "heaven." Fortunately we have found an apartment and are ready to settle in for a few months.

RIO, THE GRAY CITY

After two months in Rio, what is it really like? Well, take San Francisco, push the hills higher, remove houses and streets on the hills, then cover the hills with green jungle growth or slippery sheer rock surfaces. Squeeze all of the city into the level areas, build hundreds of high-rise apartment houses with little space in between. Then pour in four million people. That's Rio!

Now remove San Francisco's pretty flower stands and substitute magazine and newspaper racks. Take away the cable cars and substitute old motorized or electric buses, and generously sprinkle with old model cars and taxis of every description. Retain parks but don't keep them up. Then stir up the whole mélange and let it swirl.

The few traffic signals are small lights hung in the middle of the street or so fixed that neither drivers nor pedestrians can see them, especially when eyes must be alert constantly in all directions. Cars have the absolute right-of-way. Pedestrians must take their chances. How would you like to cross Market or Geary Street without signals, dodging between buses, cabs and cars, all hell bent to beat the other guy?

Take a few bona fide bums in patchy rags, toes sticking out of old shoes, perhaps a worn cap on the head, and covered with black dirt from head to toe. Give one some liquor or wine, and then he lies or falls down on the spot. Sometimes this is on the base of a statue (how about the one in front of the U.S. Embassy?), or sometimes on a little

patch of green lawn. If it is a warm evening, four or five
such derelicts may gather in a neighborhood park, talk a bit,
and then just lie down for the night. After all, Brazil's
summers are quite hot. Occasionally one falls asleep on the
sidewalk in front of your apartment house. No one bothers
about them; no one takes them away; no one really looks at
them. They're just part of "romantic" Rio.

Most of the working- or middle-class people apparently
live in apartment houses, many of which are twenty stories
high. Single houses seem to be very old and also very run-
down. After living in two hotels, we finally moved into the
apartment of one of the Institute librarians. She was taking
care of her sister's apartment for two months and so was
able to offer hers for rent to us.

The apartment has a living room, two small bedrooms,
a bath, kitchen and a tiny back porch. The kitchen is so
small (about seven feet square) that two people cannot get
into it at the same time. The sink has one cold water tap
and is too small for a dishwashing pan. So we put the dish-
pan on a small stool, the dishrack over the sink, and there we
are! Two banged-up aluminum pans are all that's furnished
for heating water or food. The supplied dishes are greasy
and dirty, requiring thorough scrubbing and rinsing before
we dare use them. Once in awhile we stop to spray or kill
cockroaches, flies or mosquitoes. The flies and mosquitoes
get to you mostly while you're asleep.

We boil water to wash our underwear and hang it up
to dry on a backporch line. For hot water in the bathroom
we light a special small water heater. What other conven-
iences do you want for $300 per month? (This was in 1966.)

It's been hard to find the kind of food we like--or
that likes us. For a country that grows coffee, they seem
to do everything to spoil the taste-- at least for us foreigners.
In the morning you receive the hot milk treatment which gives
the coffee a mud color and flavor. Coffee break comes in
tiny cups, half filled with sugar, then filled with hot strong
coffee, resulting in coffee-flavored syrup. Even the native
wine or European-type wines do not taste very good. However, a kind of apple cider called "champagne" is pleasing.
Most of the fish or meat served in restaurants is accompanied by either rice or potatoes, with no other vegetables,
no salad, just sauces. Fortunately, we had brought along
a supply of vitamin tablets to supplement the local diet.

Foreigners are advised to buy bottled water, which is called
"mineral water, " but tastes like good spring water at home.
Also, we were told not to drink the local milk.

You've been dropped into this city, not knowing the
language, without any friends, not knowing where to go or
how to get there, except by taxi. The weather is either
cloudy, rainy, or humid hot. Sightseeing is out of the question. Yet you are here to live and work and eat. You must
shop for the necessities of life and maintenance. There are
no supermarkets, no first-class shops, such as I. Magnin or
Gumps in San Francisco. Oh yes, there is one department
store, something like the former Fifth Street Store (Walkers)
in downtown Los Angeles. And there is a Sears-Roebuck
store carrying only Brazilian-made goods. But mostly there
are individual shops: Stationery, meat, shoes, yardage,
bakery, grocery, bar, pizzeria, dry cleaner, plus sidewalk
vendors. There are no doors. During business hours the
metal grille is pushed up out of the way and anyone and anything can enter, including flies, dogs, mosquitoes, dirt, odors,
bums, etc. Whatever you want, somewhere you must find a
shop that may have it, then push your way past the swarms
of people on every street.

The traffic law requires that at night you drive with
just the parking lights, or maybe only one headlight, if you
are driving in a street with lights. Buses light up the interior but have no outside lights on, unless it is a very dark
street. Then the driver may turn them on for a second.
You can hardly read the sign showing the destination, just
hope you scrambled aboard the right one. Also you have to
watch out for cars parked on sidewalks or driving up behind
you. After all, where else can a driver park?

Within two blocks of where I worked, we saw some
of the "cliff dwellers" whose shanties festoon the many rocky
hills of Rio. Two or three wooden crates had furnished the
lumber to provide a wall and possibly a roof on a ledge left
over from the ruins of an old building which once had been
built against a slope. Less than twenty feet from the sidewalk sat a character, trying to light up an old long pipe with
a flame on a straw. His "lady" companion was apparently
reclining behind the wall and peeking around the edge at the
passersby. It was quite a shock coming upon them right
downtown. In Hollywood any hills resembling those in Rio
would have been covered with expensive homes, but here the
poor squat free of charge in the world's biggest collection

of makeshift shelters known as "favelas." Each year thousands die when the rains wash everything downhill. But
soon the slopes are sprouting again wherever the "crate"
community can find a precarious toehold.

About 40 percent of the federal government offices
and bureaus have moved to the new capital, Brasília, and
little is spent by the government in keeping up Rio since all
the effort is directed to Brasília. From what we have seen,
Rio is deteriorating faster than it is being modernized, and
the filth everywhere is indescribable.

All buildings, except brand-new ones or those using
tile or terrazzo, are of a black gray color. Some say this
is soot constantly being blown from the nearby mountains.
The older the building, the blacker it is because this soot
is absorbed into the plaster and paint. From all appearances,
the buildings are hardly ever painted, so everything looks
drab. Some of the older buildings--churches, homes, man-
sions--would look quite charming if they were cleaned up and
a bit renovated. The many examples of fancy grilled iron
work in fences, balustrades, and window protectors are lost
in the general gray look of everything.

A colorful sight in Rio is a tour through the world-
famous H. Stern jewelry manufacturing company. Here young
Brazilians sit in rows, grinding and polishing fabulous gems
from the rich mines of Brazil. The state of Minas Gerais
(General Mines) is the chief source of most such stones.
After the factory tour one is shown into the sales rooms to
admire, and perhaps purchase, finished unset gems or pieces
of jewelry. Later we also visited the quaint old-style mining
town of Ouro Prêto.

If you come to Rio for a few days as a tourist, booked
at a first-class hotel, then take sightseeing trips to Sugar
Loaf Mountain, the Christ Statue, maybe out in the country
to Teresopolis, with a quick sidetrip to Copacabana for some
shopping and viewing of the beach, then you might say: 'Rio
is such an interesting place!" But I doubt that you would
want to live there.

PATTERNED SIDEWALKS

How dramatic those wavy black and white sidewalks

look in the travel folders! Some are in square patterns,
others diagonal, diamond, zigzag, floral. You name it, and
somewhere in Rio it may exist--or did at one time. The
sidewalks were constructed of irregularly shaped rocks, cut
roughly to average 1" x 2", then laid without any binding
material to form these striking designs.

These patterned sidewalks are the remnants of rock
mosaic which may have been beautiful at one time. The
driving and parking on these walks, pelting of rain, and
scuffing by careless pedestrians have altered these walks into
dangerous paths. Puddles, mudholes, missing stones, sudden
slants, exposed plumbing pipes, a pile of rocks shoved aside,
a deep hole where the lid was removed from a public utility
hole or where there is an excavation without any warning
barricades--all of these hazards require a sharp eye and the
steady arm of your companion to navigate. Sightseeing must
take second place in your attention.

Some of the huge mountains may have been leveled to
obtain the boulders from which the billions of stones were
shaped for the sidewalks of Rio. Very few places show at-
tempts at repairs. One would need all the cement in California to lay serviceable modern sidewalks, with curbs, gut-
ters, driveways. Of course, that would eliminate the "charm"
of these famous walks.

TAXI!

Apparently anyone, and almost everyone who has a car,
can operate as a taxi service. There are no taxi companies.
All it takes is a meter, a small sign on top of the car, and
a red license plate. Any old car will do--from small Volkswagens to old Chevys.

Once in the "taxi," hold on! The windows are wide
open. The vehicle becomes one of many race cars on the
wide boulevards without lanes, and anything goes. The idea
is to find any opening, no matter how slight, and zoom for
it. A determined driver who honks louder will probably
squeeze in. That's why small cars are preferred in Rio.
Cars weave back and forth and turns are made haphazardly--
just look sharp and honk! Pedestrians have no right-of-way.
If they try bravely to cross in front of a car, they are ignored.
They're expected to jump out of the way. Good luck!

Although this is frightening to anyone accustomed to
traffic lanes, controlled traffic flows, and observing minimal
driving courtesies, one tries to relax because the "taxi"
drivers seem to be gifted with a keen sense of timing as to
the give and take. Brakes seem to be good. You are delivered to your destination, sometimes with a smile. A tip
is automatically added to the fare and the whole deducted if
you give him a sufficient amount of money.

Once we met a German cab driver and I had a chance
to use my native tongue. He had been in Brazil for 48 years,
had married a Brazilian woman, had a daughter, but said he
still wasn't used to Brazilian customs, food, or thinking. He
deplored the filth, lack of organization and planning and general absence of industriousness.

Chatting with another taxi driver, we learned that
when he had turned 65, the company where he had worked
for fifteen years retired him without any pension. Since
savings are useless in an economy where inflation doubles
the price of everything every year, he turned to taxi driving
as a livelihood. He bought the smallest car possible, just
big enough for the driver and two squeezed-in passengers.

PLAY BALL!

If there's one thing my husband loves it's baseball.
And here we are, 12,000 miles from home, with the World
Series between the Dodgers and the Orioles coming up. The
league winners we know from the brief accounts in the Brazil
Herald, the only English language paper available.

But isn't there any place in Rio where we can get
either an American newspaper or listen to the games on a
shortwave radio? The American Embassy apparently has
little help to offer. The U. S. Information Library obtains
the New York Times by boat, about six weeks late. It receives the international edition by air from Paris, about two
days late, but this doesn't include any sports section. The
Institute of Bibliography Library, where I am lecturing, doesn't
receive this type of newspaper. The two biggest newsstands
in Copacabana have nothing from the U. S. A.

An advertisement in the Brazil Herald offers a used
Zenith shortwave radio for $150, and, when contacted, the

man says it needs batteries and maybe some repairs. The
big department store, Mesbla, has a new Philco battery-
operated radio for $125. Will this bring in the broadcast
from the U.S.A.? Maybe, but no one knows. Nobody seems
to have a radio we can borrow, nor does anyone care one
bit about baseball. Soccer--sim (yes); beisbol--nao (no).
Time is getting short. The very pleasant marine on guard
duty up front in the Embassy tells us that the ordinary shortwave sets cannot pull in programs from the U.S.

        A call to the Brazil Herald puts us in touch with Joe
Sims, public relations officer for Pan American. We telephone him and he seems to be a very nice and helpful fellow.
He promises to save the sports section of the Miami Herald
every day. Since his office is right next to the U.S. Embassy, we call on him.

        As we are talking, a three-day-old New York Times
arrives and he presents us with the whole paper. What a
treasure! He also gives us the name of the press attaché at
the Embassy. "Tell him Joe Sims sent you to see if you
could please listen in on the Embassy's shortwave set."

        Joe Sims is one of the ten "America's Outstanding
Young Men" for 1966, and his name is magic. The press
attaché introduces us to the radio technician, and we are
escorted to the secluded studio and communications center.

        Here, amidst a tangle of tapes, large receivers, lots
of static, is a young Brazilian who speaks some English. A
marine comes in with a list of numbers guaranteed to tune
in the Armed Forces Radio Network, originating in Ohio.
It is 6 p.m. Rio time.

        Suddenly, after some adjustments, we hear: "Drys-
dale's on second!" And there it is! The game has just
started and already the Orioles are ahead by two home runs!

        As the game progresses, the young man turns on an
amplifier in the Voice of America studio, and we can sit in
comfort, probably the only two Americans in Rio listening to
the World Series directly from Dodgers Stadium, Los Angeles,
via the Armed Forces Radio Network. Persistence has paid
off!

PROMISES, PROMISES

On the day we arrived in Rio our Fulbright Commission
host pointed out the modernistic Museum of Modern Art, at
the edge of the Bay. "That contains a wonderful restaurant, "
he said. "I've arranged for a lunch there so you can meet
some of the Rio librarians." At first we thought he meant
right then and there, or perhaps after a fast change of clothes
at the hotel. Our plane had been scheduled to arrive about
9 a.m. but was nearly two and a half hours late. At the
hotel nothing further was said about the lunch, so I assumed
it might be later in the week. After a week had gone by I
casually inquired about lunch in the beautiful Museum. "Yes,
I've been waiting for one of the librarians to return to Rio,"
he said. "As soon as she's back, we'll have a luncheon."
That was the last time the meal was mentioned, and I did
not bring up the subject again.

On the day before we left Rio, Lloyd and I finally had
lunch in that excellent restaurant overlooking the Bay towards
Sugar Loaf Mountain. Joe Sims, the personable public relations officer of the Pan American Airlines, was our guest.

Soon after our arrival in Rio, my interpreter and her
husband took us out to dinner one evening. In their little
car we drove up into the dark hills behind Rio. "It's too
bad it's dark now," she said. "In the daytime the view is
marvelous. Some time we'll show you all these beautiful
views when we get our new car, which will be bigger." We
ended up at a small café on a lonely, dark beach. When it
came time to pay for the meal, they made no move. Finally,
when we offered to pick up the tab, they did not object.

About two weeks later I asked when they expected to
get their new car. "Well, we couldn't get the Willys we
wanted, so we settled for a Volkswagen," she explained.
No further word about promised sight-seeing trips.

Another librarian at the Institute said: "I'd like to
show you some of the beautiful spots in and around Rio.
But my English isn't very good. I have a friend who speaks
good English. She's coming back next week, and then we'll
have a drive on Saturday or Sunday, if the weather is nice."
I thanked her warmly since we were rather tired of riding
street-cars and looking at highrise buildings and mountain
peaks. The next weekend was cloudy, but the following two
were beautiful--perfect for sightseeing. But--no phone call,
no car, no trip.

Since my lecturing job did not take much time, I wanted to visit as many libraries as possible. After prodding my interpreter, I was told that she had arranged a "Dutch treat" lunch with some of the municipal librarians. The day before the event she told me the lunch was postponed because one of the librarians couldn't make it. That's the last I heard of that "treat."

All of these broken promises contributed to our dim view of Rio and its people. However, towards the end of our stay a few very nice librarians redeemed the somewhat flawed reputation of the Cariocans, one by taking us on a lovely weekend trip to their mountain retreat (we saw and heard monkeys in the nearby forest!), and another by inviting us to a superb luncheon in her appartment.

NÃO FALO PORTUGUÊS!

Not knowing Portuguese is certainly a handicap. Some residents speak English, French, Spanish or German, but often only a smattering of one of these. In the little neighborhood shops and restaurants we must rely on pantomime, pointing or trying whatever words we can find in our small dictionary. A basic vocabulary of "sim" (yes), "nao" (no), and "quanto?" (how much?) can carry you through quite often.

You want cough drops in the "farmácia"? Cough and hit your chest, and lo, the attendant brings you Vicks Pastilhos. Rub your tummy and groan, and you get soda mints. I had more trouble with facial tissues. I rubbed my face, blew my nose, said "Kleenex," and "papel" (paper), but nothing got across. Later one of the English speaking girls in the office told me it's called yes. "Yes?" "Yes."

We went to a so-called Spanish restaurant and thought they might have tamales or enchiladas, even though we knew that those are primarily Mexican dishes. "Tomates?" "Não, tamales." A blank look. So Lloyd proceeded to demonstrate and explain in English. "You take some corn leaves and fill them with corn meal, chopped beef, onions and spices, roll them up, then cook them, and then--ummmmmm! Tamales!" Other waiters gathered around, but no one could figure out what it was all about. We ended up with "roast chicken," a small, tough thing with gray meat and an oily salted skin. About three bites and you're through. That's Spanish food?

We had better luck with mosquito spray. At the
farmácia Lloyd sounded a high "zzzzzzz" and then indicated
a landing on the arm and neck, with a few slaps added for
good measure. "Sim, senhor," said the clerk and, sure
enough, came back with mosquito spray.

To find a laundry, we showed our bundle of dirty
shirts to a merchant, and to find a shoe repair shop we
showed the shoes we wanted fixed. We were quickly guided,
in sign language, to the proper places. Fingers are good for
giving figures, and the cost of an item is usually handed to
you on a piece of paper, so you can read the figures.

With all these experiences, we added more Portuguese
words to our vocabulary and communication became a little
easier.

ASTRONAUTS

The two early American astronauts--Neil Armstrong
and Gordon Cooper--came to Rio on their South American
tour. We happened to be near the downtown Santos Dumont
airport just before they arrived, so we stood by the fence
to watch the proceedings. About twenty limousines of one
style or another and two open cars were lined up. A double
line of Brazilian guards in powder blue uniforms, white steel
helmets and white gloves, and with guns, formed a wide aisle
from the landing field to the cars. Photographers were on
any vantage point--ladders, steps, cars, trucks, roofs.

Soon the two-propeller airplane arrived and the en-
tourage descended. The weather was clouded over and it
was drizzling slightly. The astronauts, their wives, and
other members of the party marched through the aisle of
guards, to the welcome of a bugle call and scattered hand-
clapping. Then the motorcade began. "Hi, kids!" my husband shouted. They turned and waved, and then we scurried
off to shelter.

That noon the American Chamber of Commerce spon-
sored a luncheon for the astronauts in the Hotel Gloria. We
obtained tickets and mingled in the crowd of 300 Rotarians,
Lions, Brazilian Air Force generals, local officials, the
Governor of Guanabara, and the Ambassador of the United
States. We spotted our friend Joe Sims, from Pan American,

and chatted with him briefly. He was arranging for **Miss**
Pan American to be photographed with the astronauts, **to pro-**
mote her standing in a Miss Wings contest.

When the astronauts arrived, the Brazilian **band struck**
up the "Star Spangled Banner." Lloyd, whose **early training**
was as a tenor, burst out in song, but no one **else among** all
the Americans there bothered to join in. He got **a big hand**
and handshakes. A Brazilian gentleman came **to thank** him
and said he liked to hear the American anthem **sung.** Lloyd
managed to shake hands and speak with the **astronauts** as
they entered the dining room.

We were seated near the head table, **opposite** two
four-star Brazilian generals (one of whom was **the head** of the
Air Force) and an American one-star general. **The** meal
was cold vichyssoise, an excellent rare steak **with vegetables,**
accompanied by red wine and mineral water, **for us** a wonderful change from Brazilian food.

Intermingled with the eating were **speeches and** toasts,
while photographers vied for interesting shots. **Joe** Sims
managed to shoot the picture he wanted. **Dessert was** a
wonderful pastry with champagne for toasting **the President**
of Brazil and President Lyndon Johnson. We **chatted** with
interesting persons and had a marvelous time. **As** we left
the hotel, the sun was shining.

The next day the astronauts were **scheduled** to speak
at the Pontifical Catholic University, located **up** the street
from where we were living. We were out, **attending** to
grocery shopping at a corner stand, when sirens sounded
in the distance and drew closer.

"The astronauts!" I cried, and soon the cavalcade
was upon us. Lloyd shouted once more: "Hi, kids!" They
turned, spotted us, waved and were gone.

MAIL TO HOME

When far away from home, the need to communicate
with family and friends is intensified. Every day one looks
forward to mail from home, while letters and cards reporting on our travel experiences are sent out in a steady flow.

It is thus most disconcerting to find that there is considerable distrust of the Brazilian postal system. Everyone told us stories of nondelivery, packages lost, stamps stolen off envelopes by postal employees who are poorly paid, etc. There are no mail boxes on street corners or in business buildings. No neighborhood post offices were seen on our bus rides or when walking. We had arranged to receive our mail at the Institute as being much safer than at an apartment house.

Outgoing mail we gave to a girl in the office, who took it to some front office, where presumably it went with other outgoing mail. Repeatedly I offered to pay for the postage but was always told with a smile: "No, it is free. You don't have to pay."

One day when this girl was sick, I gave our mail to another one to take to the front office. Soon she came back and, in broken English and pantomime, told me that all addresses had to be typed, all postcards had to be put into official Institute envelopes, and then they could all go "free." She handed me all my mail from several days back, on which we had handwritten addresses. So I re-addressed everything properly, put the postcards in envelopes, gave all back to her, and asked her to please get them out TODAY.

Two days later no one was in my office to give my outgoing mail to, so I went to one of the English speaking librarians and asked her to take it to the front office, wherever that was. Again I mentioned that I was willing and eager to pay for the postage, but again she said, no, they would pay for it. Probably she noticed that I had carefully put all mail into official Institute envelopes and addressed everything by typewriter.

Soon a messenger came back with a note. "There are no stamps for your mail. It is going to take 15 days to get more stamps. If you are in a hurry, they will have to be sent by you through regular postal mail. Contact Lea."

I asked the messenger to "please take me to [your] Lea!" This turned out to be the girl in the front office who handles the mail. She handed me not only all of my latest outgoing mail, but mail for at least the last ten days, some of it even hand-addressed. It turned out that they have a postal meter machine for which the set amount of money had been used up (possibly due to our extra load of outgoing mail).

It would not be serviced for another fifteen days, so all mail was being held.

I told her I was perfectly willing to pay for our postage, and she replied: "In that case, I'll have the messenger take it over to the post office." So we paid her the proper amount and the messenger was sent on his way.

Apparently no one had informed Lea that we had offered to pay on several previous occasions. But why didn't she tell us sooner that our mail was being held up? Our family and close friends were no doubt worried at our apparent silence for two whole weeks.

NAMES AND ADDRESSES

Brazilian names have a sort of floral, literary and historical stateliness. Abbreviations are hardly ever used. and hereditary family names are liberally integrated. Often this shows a multinational background, for example: Wagner Roberto Cunha Franco, or Valter Angelo Sperling Cascato. "Wilson" and "Washington" are popular first names. Historical names with different spellings are eye-catching: Hamleto, Anibal, Guilio.

The ladies have old-fashioned names, with lyrical overtones: Amelia, Zilda, Esmeralda, Cordelia, Felisbela, Carminda, Geovana, Tereza, Heloisa, Ivanilda, Cleonice Diva, Regina Helena, Ana Cristina Pereira de Castro, Carmen Amparo Ortola Simo, Rosa Maria Martins da Cunha Guimarães, and Maria Dulce Teixeria dos Santos Castro.

Names are frequently listed alphabetically by first names rather than surnames. Three instances of this came to our notice. The first was the list of persons who had some connection with the International Overseas Service, an investment company that the government opposed. The names of investors were being listed publicly in the newspapers as a sort of warning and punishment (as well as a lucrative source of blackmail). I was looking for the name of a friend who said he had invested in this fund, and suddenly I realized that the entries were alphabetized by given name. The second occurrence was a newspaper list of students who had passed certain university examinations. The third was a book on the history of Brazilian library science. For each library school

there was a list of its professors and instructors, all listed
alphabetically by first name, from Aida to Yves, Aurelia to
Zilda, Alfredo to Terezinha.

No doubt this is due to the custom of calling people
by their first name, even among strangers. For example,
when asking for a librarian, I would ask for Dona Emy,
Dona Olga, or Senhor Alfredo. If I were to stay in Brazil
I could use the name of Dona Joãna Eleonore Voget Allerding
Tallman, to show my Christian name, Johanna, Brazilianized,
my mother's maiden name, my maiden name and my married
name.

As to addresses, there is an excellent means of deter-
mining exactly where any given address is on a city map.
It is by using a special telephone book arranged by addresses.
Under the desired street you can find the following information: the postal zone number and name of district, the cross
street or plaza where the street begins, and the last place
where it ends. Then come the address numbers, including
apartment numbers, names of subscribers and their telephone
numbers.

Wherever a cross street occurs is a large black dot
with the name of the street. So even if your friend doesn't
have a telephone number, you can pinpoint the exact location
from the closest address or a prominent building in the
block. If it is a small side street, check if you recognize
any of the cross streets. If not, merely look up the beginning of the street and see where it goes. It should now be
easy to find one of these streets in the geographical area on
the map.

This system is especially useful since street numbers
are not apt to be the same in parallel blocks. These streets
may begin at different cross streets, and all address numbering begins with numeral 1.

Another use of this directory is to locate telephone
numbers of neighbors in case of emergency or just to see
who lives in that big estate on the corner. But since this
information could also be useful to potential burglars, most
houses (especially in the better residential districts) have
fences or walls with locked gates, and dogs.

A 1984 newspaper story on increased crime in Brazil
reports that some people have turned to <u>lions</u> as house guards!

LETTER TO FRIENDS AT UCLA

December 8, 1966

Towards the end of our stay in Rio de Janeiro we managed to see some of the sights and surrounding areas. The Petrobras Co. took us to its large petroleum refinery and artificial rubber factory. These facilities are very modern and provide a large percentage of Brazil's needs in these materials. The libraries in these two places were quite special and good. About 3,000 people work at the refinery, and the company provides free transportation via a fleet of buses to various parts of Rio and suburban areas. The attractively landscaped grounds also have a pond with ducks and geese. Special facilities include a hospital, fire department and large restaurant.

Another industrial trip was to the printing and publishing company which produces all the telephone books for Brazil, as well as the Encyclopedia Americana, a Portuguese encyclopedia, many paperbacks, the Brazilian version of House and Garden, with beautiful color plates, etc. On our three-hour tour of the busy plant we were accompanied by a photographer who took many pictures. The young public relations officer who was our guide had studied at UCLA. This company also has a special library on graphic arts and related subjects.

One of our new librarian-friends and her husband drove us in their Mercedes-Benz to the mountain resorts of Petropolis and Teresopolis, the "Switzerland of Brazil." Here were lovely homes with swimming pools, racehorse paddocks, blooming gardens, waterfalls and even airstrips. At one of the local tile manufacturing places we saw Princess Ragnhild of Norway. She is married to a wealthy Brazilian and they have a big estate in these mountains. The scenery reminded us somewhat of the Santa Cruz mountains. We felt a welcome release from the tight confines of Rio's urban mountain peaks, tall buildings and narrow streets.

Our last day in Rio was sunny and hot, so we finally took the cable car trip to the top of Sugar Loaf Mountain. Both the ride and the view were real visual treats. The city of Rio shows off to best advantage from this high perch.

On December 1st we flew from Rio to São Paulo and were met by a man from the U.S. Consul General's Cultural Division. The city [along with its] immediate surrounding

Lloyd and Johanna Tallman visiting a publisher in Rio de
Janeiro, 1966.

area is supposed to have 6,000,000 people and be growing
rapidly.   You can well believe this when you see the great
crowds downtown, the traffic jams, the many modernistic
skyscrapers, the large residential areas, and the huge industrial section, where automobile manufacturers and many
other companies have large, modern plants.

        The University of São Paulo consists of seventeen
faculties or institutes.   Many of these are scattered throughout the city; only a few have been built on the new campus
called Cidade Universitaria.   It looks like UCLA in the
thirties, with lots of space, but in area it must be several
times larger than UCLA.

        A class of librarians (heads of institute libraries,
special libraries, etc.) has been meeting regularly, and I
gave a guest lecture.   One of the students is the engineering

librarian of an engineering school in the interior of the State, and he is also the dean of a library school to train librarians for the many smaller schools and cities in the interior. He has invited us to visit his school, which is about four hours by bus.

Next week we're flying to Belo Horizonte, the capital of the state of Minas Gerais. I have been invited to talk to the professional librarians in that area and visit the University Library there. So we are gradually seeing more of the country and meeting many of the librarians. They are faced with the problem of limited budgets, due to the unstable economy of the country. The budget for the University of São Paulo main library has been cut 20 percent for 1967. This makes it most difficult to modernize and improve the libraries and to raise the salaries of librarians.

So long, for now!

SÃO PAULO

Just as Rio de Janeiro is somewhat but not exactly like San Francisco, so São Paulo is somewhat but not exactly like Los Angeles. There is actually a similar rivalry and condescension between the Cariocans and Paulistans.

São Paulo is big and spread out over the countryside. There is a first-class business district, and there are wide boulevards, many lovely residential areas, and Brazil's largest concentration of manufacturing companies. The architecture of new buildings shows originality and beauty, whereas the new buildings in Rio all look alike. A large park boasts lakes, museum, exhibition grounds, eating areas, lawns, etc. Throughout the city are also many smaller, well-kept parks.

The city is located inland, about fifty miles from its port city of Santos. It is not only "in" but also "up," some 2,500 feet above sea level. This gives it a clean, healthful atmosphere, with considerable rain and wind as well as bright sunshine. Despite the heavy industry and auto traffic, there is little smog. Apparently the meteorological condition known to Angelenos as inversion layer, which helps trap smog, does not exist in São Paulo.

The major problem is lack of mass transportation.

There are motor and electric buses, but downtown streets are narrow and, at rush hours, are clogged for blocks with cars, taxis and buses. There is definite talk of a subway system in a few years. A current joke is that any large hole in the street is the entrance to the new subway.

Like Rio, and unlike Los Angeles, São Paulo has many taxis, all individually owned and/or operated. But at rush hour on a rainy night it is just as difficult to flag a taxi as anywhere else. One rainy night, after hailing cabs in vain for half an hour, we finally went to a hotel, on the theory that that would be a logical destination for some taxis. Sure enough, one came along and we finally had our ride home.

There are large department stores, fine furniture displays, dress shops that have my size, and a variety of excellent restaurants. Near our house is the newest and biggest shopping center in Brazil, the Shopping Center Iguatemi, with some seventy stores, including a three-story Sears, a large Chinese restaurant, and many specialty shops. There is even a slot-car racing arena.

São Paulo also has two rivers, two airports, and a university with large acreage, plus several private universities and schools. With all this cleaner, more up-beat and modern cosmopolitan ambience, we began to feel more at home in São Paulo than in Rio.

STOP THE BUS! I WANT TO GET OFF!

My weekly lecture class for librarians is at 6 p.m. in the Map Room of the Municipal Library, as this is a convenient time and place for them to attend. The use of taxis being rather expensive, we were glad to find that the electric bus, stopping about four blocks from the house, takes us directly downtown to the corner where the library is located.

I should explain the routine in these buses. You get on either near the rear or the middle, depending on the bus. Since practically all monetary transactions are in paper money, rather than coins or tokens, a collector takes the money and hands out the appropriate change. He also watches the passengers boarding the car and whistles an "all clear" to the driver. He sits on a sideway seat near the entrance door. Opposite his little cashier counter is a turnstile which he

activates or releases when you have paid.   If the front part
is filled and there are empty seats in the rear, one can wait
to go through the turnstile until one is ready to get off, which
must be done at the front end.

Where we board the bus is just one stop before the
bigger crowds get on, so usually we manage to find seats.
This particular evening there were no two seats together up
front but we found an empty double seat in the middle, just
before the turnstile.   Soon the remaining seats were taken
and the standees started filling the aisle.   By the time we
reached the downtown area, the bus was well packed.

As I thought "How are we going to work our way
through this mob?" I remembered that the bus terminal was
in a plaza four blocks beyond the stop where we would normally get off for the library.   So I said to Lloyd, "Let's
wait and get off at the end of the line."

But soon I realized that this bus wasn't heading towards the plaza.   In broken Portuguese I asked a lady if
the Praca de República was the fim of the linha.   She replied, "Não."   Then I knew we had to fight our way out.

Lloyd eased out of the seat and I followed him closely,
while two standees quickly squeezed into our seats.   Then
we found a solid pack of people who had no way of yielding
to let us through.   The bus driver blithely went past stop
after stop, while I hung onto the call cord.   Lloyd called
loudly in English: "My wife is going to have a baby!   I've
got to get her to a doctor!   Let me through!!   OUT!   OUT!"

Some people laughed, but no one budged.   Lloyd now
tried a rolling technique, sort of twisting and turning his
body and wedging through the wringer of humanity.   Gradually
he forced his way through.

But, alas.   I was no sylph, even if I wasn't pregnant,
and besides, I was carrying a handbag and briefcase.   I lost
sight of Lloyd and now became frantic.   What if he got off
the bus and the doors closed, trapping me for endless blocks?
So I started yelling: "I'VE GOT TO GET OUT!   STOP THE
BUS!   I WANT TO GET OFF!"

Well, I finally made it to the door, and there was
Lloyd, holding the doors back so they couldn't close, pre-
venting the bus from moving.   At last we were out.   We

reconnoitered and found we had come eight blocks beyond our
intended stop. (I always carried a city map with me so I
would know where we were if we did get lost. Thank good-
ness.)

We are now resolved to get to the front as soon as
we enter the bus, even if we have to stand all the way.
Also we want to be sure that the bus we take really does
terminate at the Praça. Or better yet, we'll take a taxi,
if we can find one.

SHOPPING ON RUA AUGUSTA

The street-car we take from our house in the suburbs
to downtown goes down a street where there seem to be many
interesting shops, so we are finally going to explore these
on foot.

Rua Augusta rises from downtown to the crest, where
Avenida Paulista, the Wilshire Boulevard of São Paulo, is
the new hub of high-rise business buildings. It descends the
hill on the other side, towards the residential areas in the
west. Excellent and attractive shops of all kinds line the steep
street. Altogether there are said to be over eight hundred,
with the better ones on the residential side. Even though
most are small by our standards, averaging twenty feet wide,
they are imaginatively arranged and decorated. It is amazing
how many different store entrances and window arrangements
can be contrived in a ten- to twenty-foot width.

The furniture stores, some of which are larger than
the popular twenty feet, contain unusual designs, with special emphasis on the beautiful reddish jacaranda wood and
supple leathers in many colors. The chair we like best is
narrow and high in the back, to support a neck cushion, and
wide in the seat, which is suspended in a hammock-like mesh.
It has soft black leather upholstery, offset by the beautifully
grained jacaranda wood frame. An upholstered ottoman comes
with this most relaxing lounge chair. Some furniture is of
molded jacaranda plywood, over which soft leather cushions
are draped, for real comfort.

We also admire large hanging lampshades, two to
three feet wide, made of heavy and colorful paper or cloth,
folded or draped into interesting shapes. These are hung

like chandeliers over dining tables or in entries. They might
make a nice souvenir as they can be folded and don't weigh
much. But the prices--$69.00 and up--put a quick damper
on this idea.

There are stores containing exquisite crystal, silver-
ware, colorful dresses, bright jewel-toned yard goods, tempting pastries and candies, fancy men's wear. We see large
courtyards of two-story galleries in buildings, where dozens
of shops open on an artfully landscaped or decorated common
center, with shiny escalators to whisk you up and down.

The Mayflower Modas, advertised in the English-
language Brazil Herald, actually does have dresses my size.
The owner speaks English and German, so I have no trouble
telling her what I like. The clothes are unusually well made,
with lining and wide French seams. I select a sleeveless
white and black dress for the hot weather, but don't like it
quite so short. The dress is lengthened another inch, at no
extra cost.

In the meantime Lloyd talks with the husband of the
owner and admires his shoes. They are ankle-high boots and
look sturdier than most of the rather dainty and feminine-
looking men's shoes popular in Brazil. He mentions a shoe
manufacturer in the next block, takes us there and introduces
us to the owner. Lloyd likes the looks of his wares and de-
cides to have a pair custom made. The man takes careful
measurements and agrees to put in a firmer arch and thicker
soles. In two weeks they are ready. They are very com-
fortable and fine looking, and cost less than $25.00.

In other shops we spot unusual art objects, gift items,
and other lovely creations, some of which we may buy just
before we leave. In spite of the Avenue's steepness and
the slippery cobblestones, we enjoyed our leisurely window
shopping tour of these specialty shops.

THE MIAMI BEACH OF BRAZIL

We were told that Brazilians, especially Paulistans,
consider São Paulo to be the Chicago of South America. And
when we took a sight-seeing trip to the port city of Santos
and adjacent areas, we were told that neighbor city São
Vicente was the Miami Beach of Brazil. It certainly looks
like it.

There are beautiful hotels and high-rise apartments, a lovely wide beach, blue ocean, with white breakers, and pretty park and picnic areas between the buildings and the beach. This is something that Copacabana Beach in Rio doesn't have. In this area is also a big lagoon, in which swimming and boating are popular.

Nearby is a popular resort island, Guaruja, reached by ferry-boat. This resort has beautiful homes, very modern hotels and apartments, and wider beaches. Many wealthy people have summer homes here, or are full-time retired residents.

On weekends the traffic is so heavy that a second road was built down the mountain from São Paulo. Now there is one road down and another up. But when very heavy traffic builds up on Sunday night, the "down" road is reversed to an "up" one, so that both roads are one way to São Paulo.

Brazil also has a "Switzerland" (Teresopolis, in the mountains seventy-five miles from Rio) and a "Niagara Falls" (the Iguacu Falls near the border of Paraguay). Brazil seems to be especially blessed not only with these scenic wonders, but also with a lack of natural disasters, such as earthquakes, tornados, and the like. When I commented on this once to a Brazilian, he replied: "Yes, it's true we have a wonderful country. Didn't you know that God is a Brazilian?"

CONGRESSO BRASILEIRO

Since 1954 Brazilian librarians have held periodic national conferences. Some 1,500 of them were expected to attend the Vth Congresso Brasileiro de Biblioteconomia e Documentacão to be held in São Paulo, January 8-15, 1967. I registered as a "Congressista," not so much to listen to lectures in rapid Portuguese, but to see how this congress differed from the national library conferences I was used to in the U.S., and to meet librarians from various parts of Brazil.

The Congress was held in a secondary school, almost in the center of São Paulo. As no school was in session (this was summer vacation), the whole three-floor building was available. There was no central point for the usual activities of registration, information, etc. Registration was in a second-floor classroom.

After filling in a form giving name, address, library affiliation and age (!), and getting a receipt for the fee of 15,000 cruzeiros (about $7.50), you took the receipt to the basement where you were given a "kit," with your name, registration number, and a few advertisements and notes.

In order to get credit for attending, you signed your name on a register, after your typed name and number, for each session. It is apparently proper to "sign in" and then NOT attend, if you want to do something else. The registers were moved every day, so you had to find out where they were, stand in line to sign, and then rush to the meeting. A certification of attendance is eventually awarded to those who signed a sufficient number of registers.

Most sessions were in the auditorium, for everyone to attend, but towards the end of the week there were smaller simultaneous sessions in various classrooms, on special libraries, reprography, audiovisual aids, etc. The program was small enough to be printed on one page.

It is customary to allow anyone to submit a paper to be presented at the Congress, as long as it is related to the specific themes of the meetings. According to one person I asked, there is no professional evaluation or refereeing of these papers, so poor ones are apt to be mixed with good ones. All papers are reproduced for distribution to attendees after the session at which they are given. I finally persuaded the girl who distributed these to give me some of the papers before the meeting, so I could follow the text and maybe get more out of the session.

The rapidity of the delivery of one of the speakers amazed me. At the rate at which she was going through the printed lecture, I realized she was just reading it at tremendous speed, with little emphasis and no dramatic pauses. However, another speaker delivered his message with strong intonations and gestures here and there, eliciting applause several times.

Very few exhibits were set up, without booths, no chairs, and often no salespeople. There were three or four book dealers, with displays of books and book-lists. Xerox, Friden, Rotex and Kodagraph, plus one or two others, represented the machine and library supply equipment manufacturers.

One unusual feature was that on the first Sunday there

was an official solemn Mass in the Metropolitan Cathedral, with the São Paulo Cardinal officiating. For Protestants a Culto Evangelico was held the following Sunday, at the Palacia das Oliveiras.

No formal lunches or dinners were scheduled. Each day a special bus took people back to the hotel downtown for lunch, returning by 2 p.m. Or you could walk three blocks to the nearest bus stop and ride to some other area where lunch could be obtained.

One of the São Paulo booksellers gave a cocktail hour one afternoon, and the famous Joquei Club of São Paulo had a cocktail party on the closing Sunday. This turned out to be a pleasant occasion. The librarians were admitted to the modern, spacious clubhouse, from which there is a magnificent view toward the city skyline, across the rich green turf, flowerbeds and the Pinheiros river. The horses and races were as exciting as at Santa Anita Park near Los Angeles.

Suddenly black clouds scudded across the blue sky. Thunder, lightning and heavy showers came sweeping by. Nevertheless, the next race was run as scheduled. Within an hour the storm had faded from the sky, and the setting sun, reflected from windows in the high-rise buildings on Avenida Paulista, provided an unforgettable finale.

A BIT OF GERMANY

While we were in São Paulo, one of my aunts wrote and suggested that I contact one of my mother's cousins who had lived in Brazil since the mid-twenties. She sent his name and address and commented: "He looks just like your Uncle Garfield." He and his wife resided in a suburb of Pôrto Alegre, called São Leopoldo, in the southern part of Brazil.

I wrote him and said we would like to visit if an opportunity arose. For several weeks there was no reply. Finally a letter arrived: "We've been on vacation and just came home and found your letter. Please come. You can stay with us. We'd love to see you."

Just about that time I attended the Congresso Brasileiro and met a librarian from the Technical Institute in Pôrto

Alegre. She invited me to visit her library there. Then a professor from the library school at the university asked me to talk to her class. When my assignment in São Paulo fell through, the Fulbright Commission in Rio encouraged me to visit libraries and travel. An inquiry about my projected trip to Pôrto Alegre confirmed that my costs would be covered, but, of course, we had to pay for my husband's expenses.

Another letter went to Cousin Gustav, announcing our coming in two weeks, and the time of our plane arrival. There was no response but we decided to go anyway. The plane arrived at 12:30 p. m. and, as I stood at the top of the ramp, I looked over the crowd and, sure enough, there was a face just like Uncle Garfield's!

As we approached him I said in German: "You must be Cousin Gustav." "Yes, yes. Your letter just arrived this morning [that slow mail system], and I hopped right on the bus to get here in time." (Our guardian angel must have been busy making all the connections!)

São Leopoldo was settled by Germans after World War I. Houses have a German look; churches were built from the floorplans of German churches; everyone spoke German. The city also impressed us with its cleanliness.

Originally Gustav had sold Brazilian leather, then set up a business making the German confection called marzipan, with almond paste imported from Germany. This was especially popular at Easter. January, the middle of Brazil's summer, is vacation time and he had no trouble recruiting teachers and housewives to help prepare the confection and package it for the Easter sales. However, during World War II it became impossible to obtain the almond paste from Germany. He tried Brazil nuts but they were too oily, so finally he abandoned that business. When we met him, he was selling yeast wholesale to bakers.

His wife, Cordelia, a Brazilian native of German descent, was the daughter of the man who first brought white grape stock from Germany to Brazil early in the twentieth century. He established the Dreher Winery, which his sons were carrying on.

In the foothills above São Leopoldo were many vine-yards, reminding us very much of our California Napa Valley. A wine festival was in progress in a foothill town. A week

or so before, the then president of Brazil had opened the
festival and the Dreher Winery had hosted a reception in his
honor.

Gustav and Cordelia drove us up to see the festivities.
The main street had booths demonstrating wine-making ap-
paratus and exhibiting various types of grapes used for the
wines. There were many opportunities to do wine-tasting.
Stores featured displays relating to viniculture, and banners
decorated the streets.

At the Dreher Winery we saw huge oak casks (in which
whiskey had originally come from Scotland), and shiny steel
vats.

"Would you like some champagne?" we were asked.

"Of course." The champagne was creamy white--a
fresh batch, not yet bubbly nor matured, but it tasted de-
licious.

"Have another!" Lloyd accepted but I thought one was
enough for me.

After his second glass, Lloyd said: "I think I'll sit
down; you go on with the tour." That champagne had a potent
kick!

We enjoyed our week in São Leopoldo, sight-seeing,
visiting a German organ factory and a wood carving shop.
In Pôrto Alegre I visited the library of the Instituto Tecno-
lógico and met, as promised, with the students at the Escola
de Biblioteconomia e Documentação da Universidade Federal
do Rio Grande do Sul.

But all too soon it was time to fly back to São Paulo.

OPERATION BANDEIRANTES

Imagine the downtown area of a large metropolis, São
Paulo, unexpectedly barricaded into rough pie-shape wedges
overnight. Cars can only enter each wedge at a checkpoint.
If your cab driver hasn't yet learned where the entrance is
to the segment where your hotel is, he will let you out with
your bags and show you the direction to the hotel. Buses

and street-cars cannot enter the downtown area. They deposit you at the rim, and then head out again, even if the street is one-way and the street-car is now going the wrong way against the auto traffic.

Large buses from outlying towns must stop at the first stop inside the city and disgorge the passengers. There are no rest-rooms, no eating facilities, no telephones. The passengers are expected to use local transportation--taxis, local buses, or street-cars. Cross-city traffic must use a designated loop road around the center.

The result is instant chaos, brought about by the newly appointed São Paulo traffic chief, Col. Americo Fontenele, backed up by police at key points. Cab drivers take advantage of the confusion to drive even more detours than necessary. A fire burns up scaffolding because the fire department cannot find the correct entry points. (We saw this ourselves.) The barricades cannot be moved--they are railroad ties and heavy timber, apparently imbedded in the streets. The only bright spot is that, once you're in the right segment, you can park anywhere, free. However, to enter in the first place, you have to pay not only a small official fee to the entrance attendant but also a tip as well.

Traffic police are needed to regulate the downtown traffic, leaving other parts of the city unprotected. Many people decided to walk, even several miles, rather than drive. The Colonel announced that a "pedestrian education campaign" will begin immediately. After that he "cannot guarantee the lives of pedestrians who ignore traffic signals," even though trucks and cars continue to go the wrong way on one-way streets or commit other violations.

Within two weeks there were anti-traffic plan meetings. The Colonel retaliated by deflating tires and blamed the mayor for not carrying out construction needed to make the plan work "efficiently." After one more week of utter distress, the Governor punctured the pride of the Colonel by giving him 48 hours to make corrections, such as in rerouting bus lines back into downtown. The Colonel decided to go on a "vacation" to Rio, saying: "Operation Bandeirantes can progress victoriously without the need for my presence." When he continued his absence, he blamed it on "occult forces." According to a news report, the people of São Paulo greeted his departure with fireworks and paper showers from skyscrapers.

We were ready to depart Brazil just when all this was going on. We were staying in a small downtown hotel and left word at the desk that we would need a large cab by 8 a.m. the next day. When we brought our luggage to the desk, no one was in sight. A few minutes later, we saw a cab driver approach the front door, but it was locked. Although we waved to him frantically, there was nothing he or we could do, so he left. Finally the clerk came. We told him that the cab had come and gone, and please get us another one! He unlocked the door, saying he would walk to the outside loop to flag a cab, since cabs no longer cruised inside the restricted zone. Then he locked the door again. We waited and waited, growing more apprehensive as we envisioned the traffic snarl which would slow our drive.

Finally he came back with another cab. We loaded up and were on our way. Although there were some traffic delays, we arrived at the downtown airport in time. We checked in and were then taken by a large bus to the international airport, miles away in the countryside.

As our big Pan Am plane took off, we heaved a sigh of relief. The plane first flew to the capital city of Brasília, then over the Amazon River and the Panama Canal to Panama City. After take-off there, we flew over the glowing volcanoes of Guatemala, making one last stop at Guatemala City. Then on to the United States, California, LAX. We were very tired but oh, so happy to be HOME!

PART IV:

RETIREMENT. WHAT'S THAT?

To many people the word "retirement" means the time when
one quits working for pay and starts drawing social security
and pension benefits. It may also mean freedom to do as one
pleases after a lifetime of paid work. Webster's New World
Dictionary defines "retire": "To give up one's work, business, career, etc., especially because of advanced age."
In the entertainment industry many never really retire; they
keep on doing what they love to do. For example, look at
Bob Hope and George Burns, both still active in their eighties!

       Actually I "retired" twice, the first time when I left
UCLA. For twenty-eight years I had contributed to that retirement system, but at age 59, when I left the university I
was too young to begin drawing that pension, which didn't
become possible until age 62. By then I was hitting my
stride in my new career at Caltech, and the State pension
was useful to build up financial security.

       When the popular retirement age of 65 finally loomed
on the horizon, I considered what to do, and when. My
health? Pretty good--no serious problems. Financial resources? Basically o.k., but inflation could deflate savings.
My job? Still plenty of challenges and administrative responsibilities. Definitely I was not ready to sit at home and
twiddle my thumbs. Besides, by continuing to work, I would
contribute more to Social Security rather than taking it out.

       Finally I reached my decision: Retire at age 67 plus,
at the end of the calendar year 1981.

From various activities which could keep me busy I
selected those that would provide an interesting balance.   For
several years I had been on the Board of Trustees of the
Pasadena Historical Society and had given cataloging data to
volunteer typists for proper indexing of the book collection.
My first choice for a volunteer job was to become more active in that area.

The first Monday morning after my official retirement
I arrived there at 9 a.m.   This sort of timing keeps up the
rhythm of arising and going to "work." So on this new "job"
I have enjoyed putting in three hours each Monday, along with
three other volunteers.   Among us all the books have been
cataloged with proper cards and subject cross-references.

For a change of pace our Monday team undertook the
indexing of the magazines which the library had accumulated
over the years.   We found many articles dealing with the
fascinating history of Pasadena, founded in 1874, known for
its annual Tournament of Roses and Rose Bowl football clas-
sics, architectural styles, and many civic and cultural clubs.
During the nineteen twenties and thirties many beautiful homes
were built, with Italian, Oriental and other special garden designs.   These were described and lavishly illustrated in arts and
architectural magazines.   Most of these homes have been carefully preserved, and present owners frequently come into the
library to learn more about the architects, previous owners,
and other details.

In early fall of 1983 there was much talk about the
forthcoming Army-Navy football game, the first to be held
in the West.   It would take place in famous Rose Bowl and
thousands of cadets and midshipmen would be flown from
the East for this exciting event.   Just about that time I came
across articles in two issues of California Life, published in
1920.   As I was reading and indexing these I became more
excited.   The articles described a football game played on
Armistice Day in Pasadena in 1920, between the Pacific Fleet
and the Western Division of the Army, in other words, an
Army-Navy game.

At a meeting of the Southern California Chapter of the
Special Libraries Association the guest speaker was Jack
Smith, famed columnist of the Los Angeles Times.   Since
he mentioned the forthcoming Army-Navy Game, I told him
briefly, after the meeting, what I had found and promised to
send him copies of the articles.   I had met him before and

he had used some of my comments in his column. So I
wasn't too surprised to read in a subsequent column:

> Johanna Tallman has retired as Caltech librarian,
> but she has not retired from remembering, or from
> knowing where the facts are filed.
> "You know this won't be the first game the Army
> and Navy have played in Pasadena, " she said to me
> the other evening after a dinner meeting of librar-
> ians at the Jet Propulsion Lab.
> ... "It isn't?" I said, not knowing what pre-
> vious game she had in mind, but knowing Johanna
> Tallman would be right.

He then reported in detail on the preparations and festivities held in connection with the 1920 game, the exciting
game itself, when 3,000 sailors marched to Tournament Park
[the Rose Bowl was not built until two years later], led by a
naval band of 130 pieces. Two airplanes tumbled and tossed
overhead, and the crowds cheered. Toward the end of the
story he finally revealed the score: Navy 124, Army 0.

Monday mornings at the Pasadena Historical Society
are still on my schedule, and other interesting stories continue to surface there. Recently the Pasadena Post Office
gave several postal record books to the Library. One records notices to carriers, dating from 1912 to 1927. A notice reads:

> All carriers (except business districts) are instructed
> to give two (2) short blasts of their whistles at
> each house or box when delivery is made. If con-
> venient and patrons prefer, two (2) short rings of
> the door bell can be given instead. March 25, 1916.

So now you know where the expression "The postman
always rings [or whistles] twice" comes from!

What about Tuesday? A friend, Alice B. Mothershead,
is the founder and long-time director of the Foreign Student
Community Liaison and Americans Abroad Center at Pasadena
City College. Students from many foreign countries attend
this excellent school, while many of the American students
like to go abroad to attend summer schools, travel, or even
study for a whole year.

Over a period of thirty years Mrs. Mothershead built

up an extensive collection of brochures, pamphlets, clippings,
books, maps, phonograph records, and other items, covering
such subjects as foreign customs, summer study abroad,
travel abroad, study tours abroad, work abroad, study abroad
for handicapped, brain drain, orientation for foreign students,
foreign student advising, and English as a second language.

This community Liaison Center Reference Library is
used by students and faculty from colleges and universities
in Southern California, by businessmen, researchers, organizations connected with international exhange programs, and
volunteers working with foreign students.

Although Mrs. Mothershead had segregated the publications in relevant groups and provided a limited index, we
agreed that I would prepare a detailed index suitable to be put
on a computer. This would include access by subject and key-
word terms, country, languages, and author. I was familiar
with a computer program designed for such a bibliographic
index.

A catalog of bibliographic data requires two major
aspects: the bibliographic data, and a filing code, similar
to call numbers for books. For the filing code I devised an
alphanumeric designation, using a letter of the alphabet for
the major categories: A, Associations and organizations;
B, Conference reports; C, Customs; through W, Work abroad.
For the numeric part we used either a straight numbering
system or a more sophisticated system to allow for a breakdown by geographical areas. For this purpose I adapted the
Library of Congress Classification for Geography (Class G).
This has a section for physical geography, which covers all
the areas of the world in considerable detail. For example,
the numbers for France and its geographical parts are GB206-
GB210; for West Germany, GB211-GB214; for Italy, GB221-
GB224. I dropped the GB and substituted a letter code suited
for the category. To expand the numerical capacity I increased
the numbers to four digits. For example, France became
2060-2109. This gave us fifty numbers for each category
having material on France. We did not go into breakdown
by parts of countries.

This system worked out quite well. Each of the items
in the library is now labeled with a distinct file number.
Most of the items are in box files on the shelves, with the
names of countries added on the box label when appropriate.
The classification brings like material together. All of the

information was put on computer card preparation data sheets. These were sent to a class learning to copy data into punch cards. After correction, these cards were converted for storage into a computer. The head of the Computer Department adapted the program I provided until we had the final format we desired. The final computer printout was run in September 1984.

Thus my Tuesday "job" has been a worthwhile project.

The rest of my week hasn't been so structured, but I'm busy. Within a week after I "retired, " I realized I missed not having a handy typewriter. So I bought an electronic one, with four "daisy wheel" discs for a variety of type styles. This has been useful in my work for several clubs.

In 1974 I had become, by invitation, a member of a service club, the Zonta Club of Pasadena, affiliated with Zonta International, an organization now with over 30,000 members in fifty countries. It is the women's equivalent of Kiwanis or Rotary Clubs and unites executive women in business and the professions in services of many kinds. The Zonta Club of Pasadena has sixty members, each representing some classification of a profession or business. Over $5,000 is raised each year by the Pasadena group for local and international service projects. On the international level, the most important is a scholarship fund named in honor of Amelia Earhart. Zonta was Amelia's only nonprofessional affiliation. Since 1938, when these awards were established, 369 awards have been made to women in 31 countries. These awards, representing a total of $1,352,400, are supported by members of nearly nine hundred Zonta Clubs. At present, each award is for $5,000 and is given to outstanding qualified women for graduate study in the aerospace-related sciences and engineering.

In 1976 I was elected president of the Pasadena Club for a one-year term and have served in some capacity on the Board ever since. My affiliation with this organization is strong, and I enjoy attending the various meetings and occasionally international conventions. As a Zontian I enjoy giving personal service once a month at the Huntington Memorial Hospital Gift Shop.

Another organization for involvement is the Fine Arts Club of Pasadena. I had been on the Board of Directors for two years when the incumbent president died, and I was

"drafted" to become the president.   This club, founded in
1913, was incorporated in 1963 for nonprofit purposes to
"encourage the creation, execution and appreciation of work
in all branches of the fine arts; to promote enjoyment of the
arts; to grant scholarship and other financial aid to deserving
artists."   Each year the club sponsors a competition for young
artists in some area of music or art.

Originally all members had to be practicing artists,
such as musicians, painters, sculptors, writers, actors.
Its honorary members have included Charles Wakefield Cadman,
Carrie Jacobs Bond (who dedicated her composition "The End
of a Perfect Day" to this club), and Gilmor Brown, the
founder of the famous Pasadena Playhouse.

The membership is limited to 150 and still includes
many performing artists.   During eight months there are
monthly dinner meetings, held in the beautiful Athenaeum,
the faculty club on the Caltech campus.   The dinners are
followed by a musical or dramatic program, as well as an
art exhibit.   In running this club I found that my experience
as president of many library organizations was useful.   Board
meetings, committees, publication of bulletins and the year-
book kept me quite busy for two years of my presidency.

Early in the 1960's information entrepreneurs were
already looking for ways to perform library-type services for
a fee.   I was always interested in becoming involved with
extracurricular activities, such as occasional consulting work,
publishing, and involvement with library associations as an
officer or committee member.

In 1964 a former UCLA engineering professor who had
established his own research and consulting company (Don
Lebell Associates) suggested to me that we set up a group of
library specialists who could provide services to engineers
and corporations.   This resulted in the establishment of an
affiliate company, called DataQuest, to provide search and
retrieval materials; literature searches; indexing, abstracting
and preparation of bibliographies; library organization and
maintenance; personnel training; consulting.   I served in the
role of adviser, in my spare time as usual.

This company did handle a number of assignments, but
eventually discontinued operation since most of us could not
devote sufficient time to the enterprise.

By the 1970's other librarian entrepreneurs who decided

to devote full-time to their "dreams" formed companies to provide a variety of information services. They found the market: companies too small to have their own libraries but in need of information and access to publications; agencies that have tremendous files which need expert indexing; new special libraries that need advice about design, organization, equipment and procedures; libraries that need fast access to large collections and want document delivery service tailored to their requirements.

Early in 1982 the president of such a company, Savage Information Services, asked me to become a member of the Board of Directors of this recently incorporated firm. Sue Savage had been a student in my course at the UCLA School of Library Service, and I had noted her upward progress over the years. After serving as the head librarian of the Douglas Aircraft Missiles and Space Systems Division in the late 1950s and early 1960s, she became involved in the development of computerized information systems--using computers to produce large databases of information that could be used by engineers and scientists within the company. She went to work for the NASA Scientific and Technical Information Facility in the Washington, D.C., area and assisted in the development of the NASA information system. She then became a consultant in the development of libraries and information systems, and in 1977 formed her own company. Her experience, imagination and business acumen enabled her to undertake such so- phisticated operation. Her present staff consists of sixteen experts in information and library services.

Examples of services that this information company provides its customers include records management of a large municipal department; development of a document control sys- tem and a tracking system for an engineering design project for an aircraft company; development of guidelines for subject control and editing of a vocabulary list for a large public utility; an extensive information control study of the central files of a large city department. The company provides a document delivery service, utilizing mainly access to UCLA's vast library collections. Through computer searches the staff can tap over five hundred on-line databases of informa- tion.

The Board meets several times a year, and I look forward to each occasion. It is a pleasure to observe the inside of this modern and successful extension of library know-how, and this association has provided me with exposure to corporate problems and procedures.

During 1982-83 I served as Vice President of a support group for the Los Angeles Public Library. This particular group is called BEST Friends, supporting the Business/
Economics and Science/Technology Departments. BEST
Friends is a nonprofit public organization formed in 1980 for
the purpose of promoting and coordinating corporate and
individual financial support for these departments. Public
libraries, including the Los Angeles Public Library, were hard
hit by reduced tax allocations, and now cannot afford necessary new--and expensive--equipment and expansion of services.
Most of the sixty members of BEST Friends are large corporations in downtown Los Angeles, represented at meetings
by their librarians.

Through monthly book sales held by BEST Friends
volunteers and through corporate donations, the group has
been able to purchase two microcomputers with peripheral
equipment. Recently this group provided the wherewithal to
set up an On-Tyme (registered trade name) electronic mail
service which may be accessed by other libraries for their
library users. This bypasses the telephones, which are usually
tied up with hundreds of calls. A new reference service called
BUSTER (Business and Economics/Science and Technology
Electronic Reference) has also been funded by BEST Friends.
This allows libraries to send brief questions via On-Tyme,
for such ready reference questions as addresses, definitions,
basic statistics, recipes, stock quotations, and checks for
availability of certain items. Photocopy requests can also
be handled in this speedy manner.

After completing my term as Vice President I decided
not to accept the Presidency because of the time involved and
the freeway drive to downtown Los Angeles on weekdays.
Also I felt that a librarian from a corporation could serve
more effectively. But I am still a supportive member of
BEST Friends.

Among other special activities in my "retirement" I
provide occasional consultation on library projects, serve
on accreditation evaluation teams, and act as election inspector
in my voting precinct. Also I have enjoyed the time needed
to sort and assemble the material for this book about my career.

All in all, retirement means a happy blend of activities
and leisure, to suit my interests. To those who fear that
retirement will be dull, I recommend becoming involved with
civic, service group, professional and volunteer services,
for satisfying later years.

PART V:

REFERENCES: WRITINGS BY
JOHANNA E. TALLMAN

1. "Training for War; a Selected Reading List," compiled
   by Eugene D. Hart and Johanna E. Allerding. American Library Assn. Booklist, v. 38, no. 19, pt. 2
   (June 15, 1942).

2. "The Pacific Aeronautical Library as a Regional Library
   in Technology." Special Libraries 36:90-92 (March
   1945). Also published in California Library Assn.
   Bulletin 6:103-104 (March 1945).

3. Joint compiler of: Subject Headings for Aeronautical
   Engineering Libraries; New York: Special Libraries
   Assn., 1949. 245p.

4. "Answer to Mr. Gull's Comments About 'Subject Headings for Aeronautical Engineering Libraries.'"
   Special Libraries 41:58-59, 69 (February 1950).

5. "The Integration of Library Service with Teaching and
   Research, in Engineering School Libraries." Journal
   of Engineering Education 41:245-248 (December 1950).

6. Compiler of: Periodical and Serial Holdings, Engineering
   Library, University of California, Los Angeles. Los
   Angeles, 1952. 70p.

7. "German and French Abbreviations and Terms Used in
   Serial Publications and in Bibliographical Citations."
   Special Libraries 43:358-363 (November 1952).

8. Joint compiler of: "Bibliography of Subject Headings Lists, 1938-1952." Journal of Cataloging and Classification 8:159-170 (December 1952).

9. "Form Subdivisions for Bibliographical Publications." Journal of Cataloging and Classification 9:25-31 (March 1953).

10. Review of: "A Recommended List of Basic Periodicals in Engineering and the Engineering Sciences," prepared by a special committee of the ACRL, PASS. In: Serial Slants 4:143-144 (July 1953).

11. "The Use of Signals in Serials Record Work." Serial Slants 6:123-130 (July 1955).

12. Review of: World List of Abbreviations of Scientific, Technological and Commercial Organizations, by F. A. Buttress. In: Subscription Books Bulletin 26:77-79 (October 1955).

13. "A Survey of Methods of Claiming Serials." Serial Slants 7:76-85 (April 1956).

14. "Accessioning." Special Libraries Assn. Southern California Chapter Bulletin, March 1956, p. 3-4.

15. Review of: American Men of Science, a Biographical Directory, 9th ed. In: The Booklist and Subscription Books Bulletin 53:129-130, 132 (November 15, 1956).

16. "Local Cataloging for an Engineering Library." Library Resources and Technical Services 1:149-154 (Fall 1957).

17. "Adequate Bibliographical Citations in Technical Literature: Rules for Writers and Users." Special Libraries Assn. Southern California Chapter Bulletin, November 1957, [3 pages], plus 2-page bibliography issued separately.

18. "The Professor Speaks, on Scientific Information, Please!" Santa Monica Evening Outlook, Dec. 6, 1957.

19. "Sputniks Pose Challenge to Technical Librarian." Santa Monica Evening Outlook, Dec. 14, 1957.

20. "Report on Documentation Symposium." UCLA Librarian,
    April 25, 1958, p.118-119.

21. "Adventures in Partial Titles." Special Libraries Assn.
    Southern California Chapter Bulletin, May 1959. n.p.

22. "Letter to the Editor, on Information Retrieval." Special
    Libraries Assn. Southern California Chapter Bulletin,
    May 1959. n.p.

23. "Panel Discussion." In: Modern Trends in Documenta-
    tion: Proceedings of a Symposium Held at the Uni-
    versity of Southern California, April 1958. New York:
    Pergamon Press, 1959, p.87-88.

24. "Are You a Serbihobbist?" Sci-Tech News 14:12-13
    (Spring 1960).

25. "Formulas for Book Stack Capacities." Sci-Tech News
    15:29 (Spring 1961).

26. "History and Importance of Technical Reports." Sci-
    Tech News 15:44-46 (Summer 1961); 15:164-165, 168-
    172 (Winter 1962); 16:13 (Spring 1962).

27. "Bibliographic Use of Serial Records." Sci-Tech News
    17:100-102 (Fall and Winter 1963).

28. Review of: Scientific and Technical Libraries; Their
    Organization and Administration. In: College &
    Research Libraries 25:438-439 (September 1964).

29. "Birth Control and Information Retrieval...." Special
    Libraries Assn. Southern California Chapter Bulletin
    27:63-65 (Spring 1966). [Controlling the proliferation
    of scientific literature.]

30. Review of: A Circular Shift Index of Abbreviations of
    Mathematical Journal Titles, by Mary L. Tompkins.
    In: Special Libraries Assn. Southern California
    Chapter Bulletin 27:79-80 (Spring 1966).

31. "Letter from Brazil...." Special Libraries Assn.
    Southern California Chapter Bulletin 28:74-75 (Spring
    1967).

32. "Physical Sciences Libraries at UCLA." Special Li-

braries Assn. Southern California Chapter Bulletin
29: 3-4 (Fall 1967).

33. Review of: Directory of Selected Research Institutes
     in Eastern Europe, prepared by Arthur D. Little Inc.
     for the National Science Foundation. New York:
     Columbia University Press, 1967. In: Sci-Tech News
     22:78-79 (Fall 1968).

34. Review of: Fundamental Research and the Universities;
     Some Comments on International Differences, by
     Joseph Ben-David. Paris: Organization for Economic
     Cooperation and Development, 1968. In: Sci-Tech
     News 22:79-80 (Fall 1968).

35. Review of: PB-AD Reports Index; BSIR, BTR, USGRR,
     USGRDR 1946-1967, compiled by Nina Bradshaw.
     Washington, D.C.: Technical Information Service,
     1968. In: Sci-Tech News 22:113 (Winter 1968).

36. Review of: Regional Access to Scientific and Technical
     Information; A Program for Action in the New York
     Metropolitan Area, by Russell Shank. New York: New
     York Metropolitan Reference and Research Library
     Agency, 1968. In: Sci-Tech News 23:22 (Spring 1969).

37. Joint compiler: Periodical and Serial Holdings. 2d.
     ed. Los Angeles: Engineering and Mathematical Sci-
     ences Library, University of California, Los
     Angeles, 1969.

38. "Introduction to Serials Indexing and Abstracting Servi-
     ces." On-The-Job Training of Library Personnel.
     Santa Monica: System Development Corp. TM-3962/
     001/00. October 31, 1968, p. 48-77.

39. "Salary position paper." Goals for UCLA Librarians.
     Los Angeles: UCLA Librarians Association, 1969.
     p. 5-12.

40. "The Sci-Tech Tack; from the Chairman's Quarter."
     Sci-Tech News 23:69, 104 (Fall and Winter 1969).

41. California State Library. State Technical Services.
     Library Service to Industry; Series of Four Workshops.
     Sacramento: California State Library, 1969. Re-
     marks by J. Tallman included in p. 67-159.

42. The New Management Network at the University of Cali-
     fornia, Los Angeles. Distributed by the Office of
     the Librarian, 1969. 8p.

43. "Manual Classed Order Filing, Combined with Internally
     'Divided' Catalog." Special Libraries Assn. Southern
     California Chapter Bulletin 32:165-170 (Summer 1971).

44. "Sources of Technical Information." Proceedings and
     Papers of the Symposium on Information Sources for
     Career Exploration, published in: News Notes of
     California Libraries, Winter 1971 supplement, p.319-
     324.

45. "The History of Technical Reports, 1700 B.C. to Date,
     with Interesting and Humorous Sidelights Encountered
     on the Way." Paper presented at the First Annual
     Universal Resources Information Symposium, North
     Hollywood, February 23, 1972. 17p.

46. "The Cooperative Academic Libraries Feasibility Study;
     the Point of View of a Small Library." California
     Librarian 35:12-17 (January 1974).

47. "An Affirmative Statement on Copyright Debate." Ameri-
     can Society for Information Science. Journal 25:145-
     150 (May-June 1974).

48. "The Family of 'Electronics World.'" Title Varies
     1:29, 31-33 (September 1974).

49. "Letter to the Editor." Network 2:3, 32 (April-May
     1975). [On the use of cross-references in a library
     catalog.]

50. "How the Flow of Information Could Turn into a Dribble,
     and Some Solutions to the Problem." IEEE Society
     on Microwave Theory and Techniques. Newsletter,
     Spring 1975, p.12-13.

51. "Letter to the Editor." Sci-Tech News 30:7 (January
     1976). [On the word "chairperson."]

52. Review of: University Science and Engineering Libra-
     ries: Their Operation, Collections, and Facilities,
     by Ellis Mount. Westport, Conn.: Greenwood Press,
     1975. In: College and Research Libraries 37:185-
     186 (March 1976).

53. "The Budget Pinch; Coping in University Libraries."
     Managing Under Austerity; a Conference for Privately
     Supported Academic Libraries. Summary Proceedings.
     Stanford University, 1976. p.53-65.

54. Review of: Science and Engineering Literature; a Guide
     to Reference Sources, by H. Robert Malinowsky. 2d
     ed. Littleton, Colo.: Libraries Unlimited, 1976.
     In: College and Research Libraries 38:69-70 (Janu-
     ary 1977).

55. Review of: The Management of the Information Depart-
     ment, by Denis V. Arnold. London: Deutsch, 1976.
     In: Information Processing and Management 13:262
     (1977).

56. "Implications of the New Copyright Law for Libraries
     and Library Users." IEEE Transactions on Pro-
     fessional Communications, PC-20/3:178-184 (Novem-
     ber 1977). [Paper given at 1977 IEEE Conference
     on Scientific Journals, Reston, Virginia, May 4, 1977.]

57. Review of: Information Work with Unpublished Reports.
     London: Deutsch, 1976. In: Information Processing
     and Management 13:261 (1977).

58. "Letter to the Editor." Journal of Academic Librarian-
     ship 3:158-159 (July 1977). [On copyright questions.]

59. "One Year's Experience with CONTU Guidelines for
     Interlibrary Loan Photocopies." Journal of Academic
     Librarianship 5:71-74 (May 1979).

60. Review of: Budgetary Control in Academic Libraries,
     by Murray S. Martin. Greenwich, Conn.: JAI
     Press, 1978. In: Special Libraries 70:309 (July
     1979).

61. "What Is an Engineering Librarian?" Queen City Ga-
     zette (Special Libraries Association, Cincinnati, Ohio),
     no.2, 1979-80, p.21-22 (September 1979).

62. "Perils of Publishing." Title Varies 6:9, 11 (March
     1980).

63. "The Impact of the OCLC Interlibrary Loan Subsystem on
     a Science-oriented Academic Library." Science & Tech-
     nology Libraries 1:27-34 (Winter 1980).

ABOUT THE AUTHOR

Johanna Eleonore Allerding was born in the city of Lübeck in northern Germany in 1914 and immigrated to the United States with her parents and older sister in 1923. In 1924 the family settled in Los Angeles.

After attending Los Angeles City College for one year, Johanna transferred to the University of California in Berkeley. By that time she had already decided on a career as librarian. Graduating with a B.A. degree in French in 1936, she obtained admission to the University's School of Librarianship, which offered a one-year postgraduate program. At that time the University called the degree a Certificate in Librarianship, although it was considered the equivalent to the Master's degree being given elsewhere.

Graduating during the final years of the Depression in 1937, she managed to find positions which led to her interest in scientific and technical librarianship. In 1945 she became the head of the newly created Engineering Library at the University of California at Los Angeles. Advancing to become Coordinator of Physical Sciences Libraries in 1963, she also participated in the founding of the School of Library Services at UCLA and subsequently taught classes on the literature of science, engineering, and technology.

In 1954 she married Lloyd Anthony Tallman. In 1966 she was asked to go to Brazil for six months on a Fulbright Grant to lecture on scientific documentation. She and her husband thoroughly enjoyed this change of pace and the experience of living in a foreign country. After eighteen years of a happy marriage, Mr. Tallman died in 1972.

In 1973 she became the Director of Libraries at the California Institute of Technology, where she remained until her retirement at the end of 1981.

Johanna Tallman has served in many professional organizations, among them: Council of the American Library Association; Chairman, Engineering School Libraries Committee, American Society for Engineering Education; President, Southern California Chapter, Special Libraries Association; Chairman, Southern Section, California Academic and Research Libraries, California Library Association; and President, Librarians Association, University of California. More recently she has been the President of the Zonta Club of Pasadena (affiliated with Zonta International); President of the Fine Arts Club of Pasadena; and has served two terms as a member of the Board of Trustees of the Pasadena Historical Society.

Among her advisory services to government and other agencies and corporations, she served as Director, Recataloging Project, U.S. Naval Ordnance Test Station, China Lake and Pasadena; Member, Advisory Committee, Los Angeles Trade Technical College, for curriculum for library assistants; Member of Evaluation Teams, Western Association of Schools and Colleges; and consultant to various universities and corporations, including the Colorado River Board, Beckman Instruments, Lockheed Aircraft Corporation, Capital Research and Management Co., University of Arizona, University of California at Davis, Irvine and Santa Cruz; and the Jet Propulsion Laboratory. Currently she is a member of the Board of Directors of Savage Information Services, a successful corporation providing specialized information and library related services to governmental agencies, corporations, libraries, and individuals.

She is listed in Who's Who in America; World Who's Who of Women; Biographical Directory of Librarians; Who's Who in the World; Who's Who of American Women.

INDEX